WHEN THE SIRENS SOUNDED
A Wartime Childhood

by
K . M . P e y t o n
(K a t h l e e n H e r a l d)

WHEN THE SIRENS SOUNDED
A Wartime Childhood

by Kathleen Peyton

Published by AAPPL Artists' and Photographers' Press Ltd.
Church Farm House, Wisley, Surrey, GU23 6QL
info@aappl.com   www.aappl.com

Sales and distribution, UK and export
Turnaround Publisher Services Ltd.,
orders@turnaround-uk.com

ISBN 9781904332701

Printed and bound by CPI Group (UK) Ltd, Croydon, CR0 4YY
Cover and content design by Cameron Brown cmb@aappl.com
and Stefan Nekuda office@nekuda.at
Set in Goudy Old Style

To all my friends at
Wimbledon High School

ONE

They came from the council to fit us with gas masks, my mother and father, my brother Peter and me. Peter and I got the giggles, we couldn't help ourselves. We looked so funny with our black snouts sticking out and Peter had already learned at school that if you breathed out very hard you could make a wonderful rude noise out of the sides by your ears, which he insisted on doing. I tried as well. We sat there snorting and laughing and the mica eye-pieces steamed up and we couldn't see a thing. My mother got cross.

"This is serious, for goodness sake! Behave yourselves."

The mask came in a square cardboard box with a strap to go over your shoulder.

"You must take it everywhere with you, every time you go out. You must never leave it out of sight, never," the lady said.

"Golly," I thought, "What a bore."

"And the Anderson shelter will be delivered next week, and it's up to you to erect it."

This was directed at my father.

"We suggest the hole should be at least six feet deep."

My father didn't do digging. It was our mother who was the gardener, but he
nodded politely. We had already discussed the pros and cons of being evacuated ---- just Peter and me, of course --- but thank goodness our parents had decided against it. "If we go we all go together," my father said. Meaning die. We didn't live right in London, after all, just in the suburbs to the South West. There was a lot of concrete and new

by-passes all round us but on our bikes Peter and I could be in the country fairly soon, six miles or so. We went nearly every weekend to the farm of his best friend Freddie.

My brother was twelve and I was ten when war was declared. We heard the news on the wireless and Peter and I were thrilled to bits, thinking of the excitement, but my mother cried, which we'd never seen before. It was only just over twenty years since the last one finished and all her boy-friends had been killed so I suppose that was what she was thinking. Our father was too old to be called up so that was no worry. He was quite old. I went on the train farther into London, to Wimbledon, to school. The school had already evacuated itself into Dorset, but those who didn't want to go could stay. Most went, but about a hundred of us stayed in our slimmed down school. When we all got our gas-masks of course we had to have a gas mask practice.

"When the bell goes, we will all put on our gas-masks and file in an orderly fashion down to the air-raid shelters."

We had already practiced filing in an orderly fashion down to the air-raid shelters, and had done it several times when it wasn't a practice at all but the real thing. This was when the sirens went. No bombs had dropped but there had been a lot of noise from the anti-aircraft guns up on the common so presumably there had been something up there to fire at. We had all secretly hoped for a bomb on the emptied school but no such luck. The day of our first practice with the gas-masks didn't really go according to plan. Our teachers had to put theirs on too, and of course when they had them on no one could hear what they were saying, so the orderly file down the stairs to the garden became something of a riot. Because we were all snorting to make rude noises and turning quickly to crash our snouts together and laughing so much, all our eye-pieces steamed up and we couldn't see a thing, so several girls fell down the stairs and the others behind fell over them at the bottom and in the end we had to take our masks off and get gassed in order to find out what we were doing. The teachers took theirs off and roared at us, and then we all put them on again and order prevailed.

The air-raid shelters had been dug by workmen, not our fathers, in long lines in the school garden. They were sunk in the ground and roofed with hoops of corrugated iron topped with earth. We sat on benches in two lines facing each other, knees touching. The teacher sat at the top. It was hard enough to see in the dim lighting and to hear if you were at the bottom, and with gas masks on it was impossible because no one could hear what the teacher was saying and we were all steaming up with laughter all the time. So that was the only practice we had with gas masks.

6

But we still had to carry the beastly things everywhere. Except for Annabel. Her father said it was unnecessary to carry a gasmask. The school did not argue. They never argued with Annabel's father.

My father meanwhile dug his hole at the top of the garden, but it wasn't very deep. My mother took his photo posing in the entrance, but he was kneeling down, so it looked quite deep in the photo. It had its hoop of corrugated iron, courtesy of the council, over the hole and my mother's poor flower beds heaped on top and my father made two bunks at ground level for himself and my mother. These were hinged to a wooden frame round the top of the hole and lifted up so that Peter and I could drop down into the bottom of the hole, then laid back in place, touching. The hole was only two metres square so very squashy. Of course my parents weren't going to sleep there unless the sirens went but Peter and I had to go down there every night to do our homework and go to sleep. The walls were slimy clay and although we had plenty of stuffing underneath us and a torch each it was terribly cramped and freezing cold and horrible. When the sirens went my parents came down but they only sat up there and talked and my father smoked, until the all clear went. Usually it was quite noisy with all the guns going in the local recreation park and the intermittent noise of aircraft, and sometimes we had bombs which was very exciting, but our parents wouldn't let us out to see. They were incendiary bombs, quite small but very dangerous as they set off fires all over the place. All the adults in the road had to take it in turns every night to do air raid duty and I think my parents quite enjoyed it. One night they had to go next door and put out a fire. My father came back laughing.

"Mr Horton's armchair was on fire. He just stood there shouting. I put it out with his soda water syphon."

"Pity he wasn't in it," I heard my mother say.

Sometimes when the All Clear had sounded we were

allowed out to go upstairs to our bedrooms to look out of the windows to see the terrible glow of the fires over London. This was no joke at all and our father said we will never forget this.

That was true, as I haven't.

Sometimes we had raids in the daytime and my mother would shout at us to run down to the shelter. But we used to caper about on the lawn, wanting to see the bombers. Against a clear blue sky they came in formation, high and elegant like a skein of geese.

"What are they?" my mother asked Peter.

"Heinkel one elevens," Peter said. He could recognize every aeroplane, ours or theirs.

"Get in! Get in!" screamed my mother.

We all jumped into the hole together. Sometimes the bombs came, with an eerie, crescendoing whistle and we would get our windows blown in and the ceilings got covered with cracks, but that was all. My father said Peter and I did worse damage playing cricket or football. We did break the windows at times. Of course we quite soon forgot to take our gas masks everywhere we went and we got used to the raids and used to cycle out to the farm at weekends just as usual and go to the pictures as we normally did. In the cinema everyone just went on watching when it came up on the screen that the air raid siren had just gone. I never saw anyone walk out.

But just sometimes, although utterly forbidden, Peter and I would sneak out after a raid and go on our bikes to look and see where the bombs had fallen. We only did it once or twice. It wasn't very nice at all, seeing the men digging in the rubble and people with blood all over them and women crying. We didn't do it again.

TWO

To go to school I used to catch the eight-thirty-five train from the local station which was a ten minutes walk from home. All the same people used to disgorge from their houses every morning and I used to judge the moment to slip out in order to avoid the ones I didn't want to walk with. I knew mostly they didn't want to walk with me either but we were all very polite and if you got it wrong you were forced to make the journey with a city gent in a bowler with rolled umbrella. There was a Mr Van Rood who wore spats and another girl from our school who I made sure I missed, and a lady secretary called Gwenda who I didn't mind. As I was always a horse on these occasions, I preferred to do the journey alone, so that I could go from extended walk to working trot into collected canter as I wished, talking softly to my horse. I usually threw in a few bucks and shied at pieces of paper in the gutter if there was no one behind me. I chose a different horse every day out of an exercise book I kept with over a thousand horses listed. I had a close friend at school called Triggy who was also a horse and she too had a large stable in her exercise books, so when we got to school we exchanged notes as to who we were riding and at break we did a little schooling in a corner of the playground. We pawed the ground in prayers, which got us a puzzled admonition from the nearest teacher. She had no way of knowing we were horses.

I always stood in the same place on the station and my friend Anne from farther away stuck her head out for me and we sat together revising our homework. Anne wasn't horsey and was my only non-horsey friend. We used to see a lot of each other out of school because we lived close and I loved going to her house which was enormous and her parents were lovely, much nicer than mine. Her father used to let me play his gramophone and all his records. At home we only had Tubby the Tuba and my father's scratched "The Music Goes Round and Round and it Comes Out Here" which I didn't like. I bought Finlandia, but sat on it quite soon, which upset me a lot.

Anne's parents were religious and so she wasn't evacuated, as whatever happened was God's will. The same applied to Biddy, and I suppose myself, although in my case it wasn't God's will, but Fate. After all, even if you were evacuated you could get killed. A lot of children were sent to America and some of the ships they were on were torpedoed, so that didn't do them any good at all.

One morning when I was going to school the siren went. Of course we all took no notice and stood on the platform waiting for the train, a bit edgy I suppose but pretending we weren't. The station was high up on an embankment with the sewage farm below on one side and a road running down to it on the other with a few new shops straggling at the bottom. The bowler hats were all reading their copies of the Times as usual. The train came in just as the noise of aeroplanes came to our ears, not bombers, but fighters which were quite different. Anne was sticking her head out so I got in her carriage and sat down next to her and as the train moved out we heard the sudden clatter of machine gun fire.

The carriage was full of bowler hats as usual and they all leapt up and shouted at Anne and me: "Under the seats, children! Quick! Quick!" They shoved us bodily down and all crashed down on top of us but in the same moment the machine gun stopped and there was no noise at all except for the plane whizzing away up into the sky and the train bowling along to the next station. Of course Anne and I got the giggles and although we tried to stop ourselves we were in agonies of repressed snorting for the rest of the journey. The men got up and went back to reading their papers as if nothing had happened and when we thankfully got out at our station we let go our mirth and rolled about the platform helpless. We seemed to get the giggles very easily.

Anne was a very altogether girl and never took sides amongst the cliques in our class and was nice to all the girls nobody liked and was never bullied by Annabel so she came to take the part of arbitrator in all the rows. She also liked fat so ate everybody's fat at our table in school dinners which was jolly useful. We would cut it off and pass it under the table to her in our fingers. We used to have boiled rice

with a dob of golden syrup on top for pudding and I couldn't eat this and had to sit alone with a teacher until I did, and Anne had gone by then but I knew she would have eaten it for me if she could. I used to cry and my gorge rose, but it was no good, I had to eat it. I tried to be sick, but couldn't quite manage it unfortunately.

One day when we had been in the shelters all day and it had been very noisy, Anne and I left school to go home and when we got to Wimbledon station we found there was just a big hole where the entrance was and the rest of the station was cordoned off.

We asked a porter what to do and he said it was no good waiting for a train out of Waterloo. "They've bombed the flyover. You'd better go and find a bus."

Of course there was a huge crowd for the buses and we had to wait for ages and but eventually we got pushed on and we didn't have to pay. The bus was going to not very near to where we lived but only nearer. I got off where I thought was nearest and walked miles along dreary suburban streets to home but it was a long walk, and going dark. I felt terribly sorry of myself and cried as I walked along, and when I got home at last my mother was beside herself with worry which expressed itself in a terrible rage.

There was no way I could have told her, as we didn't have a telephone, but not long afterwards when my father's office in Westminster was bombed flat we got a telephone, as he moved his office into the spare room at home. I wasn't allowed to use it of course, only to ring Pam Wright when I couldn't do my algebra homework and was in floods of tears near to bedtime. My mother would get fed up, she was no good at algebra. Pam Wright would tell me how to do it in a flash and all would be well. Pam Wright must have got a lot of phone calls, I often thought.

The trains were running again in the morning with planks over the holes at the station so unfortunately we didn't miss any school.

I was very lucky when it came to the pecking order in our class. I had nothing special going for me (except I could draw the best) but I was best friends with Annabel who was top of the pecking order in our class, only because I was horsey like her, and best friends with Anne because we were thrown together by where we lived. I was also quite friendly with the third bunch, the girls who were in the hockey and tennis teams and played Hamlet and Macbeth, etc. in the school plays, girls of strong and fine character (I got Nerissa and Audrey in Shakespeare and other inferior parts) and also quite friendly with the very clever quiet ones who subsequently became dons and doctors and chairpersons of the Women's Institute. I was a sort of all-rounder but mostly ignored as hopeless in an offhand way because of my total horsiness. My total horsiness was inflamed by frustration, as I scarcely ever saw a horse and never rode one and lived only for the horses of my imagination which were stabled in my exercise book with all their looks and habits written out a great length. Why I was born like this I had no idea. No one in my ancestry was horsey. My grandfathers were a tobacconist and a linguist respectively and my father an engineer, my mother a shorthand typist (for my father, the boss, whom she later married. Very romantic, as in a women's magazine).

I knew Annabel despised me, as she did nearly everyone, but as I hung on her every horsey word she endured me with good grace. For Annabel was a star rider who rode in shows and had lessons in expensive private stables with famous show-jumpers. She was big and gorgeous with flashing white teeth and expertly coiffed blonde hair. She got time off for horse-shows, with a note from her father which the school swallowed. If the school ever complained about Annabel --- once, the only time they dared, for not wearing socks with her sandals in the summer ---- they got very short shrift from her father. He was the only parent who took sides with his child. All other parents, mine included, took sides with the school in any complaint. They never dared suggest, unlike Sir Ambrose Horkesley, that their child might be innocent. One got punished twice over, once by the school and secondly from one's parents. Annabel got hopeless results as she didn't care and had so much time off, but nothing was ever said. Nobody hated Annabel: it was just accepted that she was on another planet from the rest of us.

I actually didn't like her very much, but she was my best friend.

My other horsey friend was Biddy who lived out in the country, and rode imaginary horses like me. My other best friend was a very clever girl called Triggy with whom I read Biggles books and talked about aeroplanes.

* * *

My mother said, "There's new people moving in across the road. No children. A retired couple. They've got a nephew who lives with them when he's on leave."

"What's he in?" Peter asked.

"The Air Force."

I perked up at that. I was into the Air Force, because of knowing all the planes and reading Biggles books all the time. I was going to be a WAAF when I was old enough (Women's Auxiliary Air Force) but everyone else in our school was going to be a WREN (Women's Royal Naval Service) because the uniform was much the smartest, navy-blue with a white shirt and navy tie and a very smart hat. If you were a WAAF the uniform wasn't so hot but you could fly planes. You delivered them from the factory, Hurricanes and Spitfires.

"Is he a fighter pilot?" They were the creme de la creme.

"In bombers, I think they said."

"A pilot?"

"I don't know. By the way, Miss Eburne wants to see you. She wants you to collect National Savings for her."

This was directed at me. I made a face. We all had to do things for the war effort and one was supposed to work with a will. At school we had to knit. I had knitted one half of an RAF pullover with Triggy but I knitted rather tightly and she knitted loosely and when we came to sew it together it looker very peculiar. I was a bit worried at the thought of a heroic pilot opening his parcel and trying on our pullover. We'd done our best though. We always knitted in lessons if it was only listening. But all Peter did for the war effort was play the euphonium in his school's Air Force Cadet band, which he really liked (I cleaned it for him and he gave me sixpence). Nobody asked him to collect National Savings.

This entailed calling on people's houses in the road and selling them stamps, sixpennies (blue) or half-crowns (red). It was organized by a woman called Miss Eburne up the road. Miss Eburne was glamourous and rather posh. She hadn't got a job; she looked after her elderly parents and they lived in a nicer house, not a semi. It had garden at the sides. I called on her as ordered and she came to the door and asked me in. She wore a very smart pale blue costume and lots of make-up. She had glistening white teeth and very blue eyes. I thought she was beautiful. What a pity she was an old spinster! Everyone was sorry for her. She was nearly thirty. But she was very kind and, best of all, she took a magazine for posh people called the Tatler. On its sports pages it had the most beautiful photos of horses, mainly the racehorses that belonged to the Aga Khan or Solly Joel, and pictures of Lady somebody using her old hunter in a trap to collect salvage, or some famous ex-Oaks winner all rough and muddy with a foal. In return for my services Miss Eburne would cut all these pictures out for me and give them to me every Sunday when I went back with the money. I kept a horse scrap book but mostly it was newspaper cuttings which soon showed the glue through but the Tatler ones were shiny and clear and beautiful and I was very pleased with them.

She said to me, "Eleven is a bit young to have charge of so much money, but you're very sensible. You have to do it on Sunday mornings because that's when everyone is in, but on Sunday mornings all the other girls go to church. And the boys are so careless."

When I sold the stamps, mostly I just stood on the

15

doorstep while the person went and fetched the money. It was quite difficult tearing out the stamps and taking the money and having to give change especially when it was freezing cold and my fingers were numb, but one or two people asked me in and the nicest of these were the couple who lived directly opposite our house, Mr and Mrs Andrews.

The first time I called I already sort of knew them, but I'd never been in their house before. It was like ours, not like Miss Eburne's, and smelled of pipe smoke and their dog and the Sunday dinner cooking. There was a photo of a young man in Flight Lieutenant's uniform on the sideboard and on my first visit I gazed at it, stunned. He was heavenly.

"That's our John," Mrs Andrews said as she scrummaged in her handbag for the money. "Our nephew. He's in bombers, doing his tour over Germany just now. He'll be back here for a week or two when he's finished."

She laughed. She was plump and motherly, although she had no children of her own. She had grey curly hair and went out to work, which was fairly rare in our road.

"He's a right laugh. Always stirs us up, doesn't he, love?"

Mr Andrews agreed that he did.

"He was my sister's lad -- but she died a while back, so he's like our own now."

The houses opposite were new, which is why I didn't yet know about who lived where. Ours had been there since I was born. We missed the field opposite for playing in when it was built on, although the building site and half-finished houses and scaffolding and piles of sand had been a great playground for the last year or two. I had been in Mrs Andrew's house before it was finished, cooked sausages in the very grate before which I was now politely sitting.

John was twenty, I learned, and had lots of girl-friends.

"You'll meet him when he comes home, I tell you, he's a right laugh."

16

I went home and told my family all this. Nobody was very impressed.

My mother said, "How much money did you collect?"

And my brother said, "It's your turn to feed the rabbits."

My father didn't say anything. He was in the garage, tinkering with the car which he did most weekends. We were the only people in the road who had a car because my father did work of national importance (he was a hands on engineer who looked after reservoirs and waterworks when they went wrong). He had bought the car off Mr Temme a twenty-stone Channel swimmer and it was always down on one side, which he was having a job to rectify.

So I took the money back to Miss Eburne and she cut me out a picture of Owen Tudor winning the Derby and one of Lighthouse the Second from a last year's magazine and I went home and stuck them in my scrap-book. Then I had to go and pick rabbit food on the railway embankment before it went dark.

THREE

We were having tea at the dining-room table, Peter and I only had fish paste sandwiches as we both had school dinners when outside in the road there was suddenly a lot of hooting, shouting and laughing and when we went and looked out there was this little red MG sports car with no top and this wonderful man in uniform pulling a rather buxom blonde Waaf out of the passenger seat. He pushed back his cap showing curly dark hair, and I could see he was just as handsome as in his photograph. The blonde was giggling and giving little shrieks as she got hung up in a bag of golf clubs. She had peroxide hair and lots of lipstick and looked as if her uniform was a size too small. Mr and Mrs Andrews came out and ran down the garden path and there was a lot of embracing and chattering, very noisy for our road and you could see everyone looking out through the net curtains wondering what the commotion was. John started heaving suitcases out of the car. He was tall and slim and very active in his ways. I goggled after him as went up the path with Mrs Andrews. They all went in and quiet reigned again.

"Well," said my mother doubtfully.

It was Friday. On Sunday morning if I was lucky I would meet him. If he didn't go out with his blonde. I would go early. Not too early or he might still be in bed. I was thinking this when the siren went.

"Oh, not already!" my mother said crossly.

Usually it went when it got dark.

"Off you go. You can take the cake with you."

Peter and I trailed down the garden with the cake and

sat on the shelter steps, eating.

"I wonder what he's in," Peter said.

"Bombers."

"What though? Wellingtons, I suppose."

"How many crew have they got?"

"Five. Pilot, co-pilot, navigator, wireless operator and gunner."

"Who drops the bombs?"

"The navigator. He's supposed to know they're in the right place."

"How does he know?"

"He navigates, stupid. They fly on a compass course, and estimate time and distance, and allow for the wind, and pick up landmarks, rivers and things, and when they get there they drop flares to light up the target. And all the time they're being shot at and they mustn't alter course or fly away, not till they've dropped their bombs in the right place."

I sat there thinking about it. I could hear the bombers now, their bombers, and thought of the Jerries up there having navigated from Germany, looking for London. If they were over us they would be too far to the West. But they would see the railway line going into Waterloo and shortly after that the river Thames and if they had any sense they would turn right and follow them into London. Poor London. But quite often the fighters and guns gave them such a hustling that they dropped their bombs anywhere, which could quite well be on us. Peter and I always assumed they wouldn't, being optimists by nature. We only went into the shelter because our mother made us.

The All Clear didn't go and my mother decided we might as well settle in for the night, with our homework, so we got our pyjamas and sleeping bags and torches and got down in our hole and I did my French and most of my algebra and Peter read the Hotspur. (He didn't work very hard). Our parents were out in the street fire-watching. When they came in just before dawn they sat on their bunks talking and smoking and I heard my mother say, "Funny, that John across the road was quite frightened. He said he'd far rather be up there dropping them than down below receiving them."

"And yet he's been shot down, Mrs Andrews said."

"Yes, they had to make a crash-landing on the coast somewhere, came back on one engine and the gunner killed."

The next day John took his Waaf out in his car all day. They both wore civvies and I watched them go, out of the bedroom window. John wore grey flannels and a brown tweed jacket and a cream shirt with a silk scarf in the neck and looked fantastic. I couldn't take my eyes off him. Of course uniform always looked more fantastic and sometimes civvies were a terrible let-down, but not in John's case. He looked very clean and athletic, the sort my mother liked. His Waaf looked very tarty in a bright red costume with white frills at the neck, white gloves and black high-heeled shoes, and her hair was on top, not very firmly. I thought the MG would demolish it quite soon but she tied a bright green headscarf over it before they set off.

I don't know where they went. I thought about them all day.

The next day, Sunday, I went and fetched my stamps early. John's MG was parked outside and I called at nine-thirty, which I thought was late enough to be up, but too soon to be about to go out. While I was standing on the doorstep I could smell bacon frying, a good sign, I thought.

Mr Andrews came to the door.

"Come in, lovey. You're early this morning."

I didn't explain why. There was no sign of the Waaf but I could hear John singing "I never thought that I should ever see, A thing so lovely as a tree" upstairs. I thought the bacon was probably for him (his uncle's ration) and my timing impeccable.

Mrs Andrews came in with her handbag and said, "We're all at sixes and sevens. Don't mind us. It's John and that girl of his, like having the whole Air Force in. I think we need a certificate, dear."

I got my notebook out, very slowly.

The singing stopped, then started again on "Pale hands I love, Beside the Shalimar." My father sang that in the bathroom too.

I fumbled for the stamps. Mrs Andrews had her money ready, five shillings. They were big savers. I tore off two half-crown stamps and took the money, a ten shilling note. Because I had called on them first I had no change.

"Have you got change, love?" Mrs Andrews asked her husband.

"No. Only two sixpences."

Mrs Andrews went to the stairs and called up, "John, have you got any half-crowns? We want some change."

And the singing stopped and he came bounding down the stairs. He wore navy-blue silk pyjamas and a silk Paisley dressing-gown and he was freshly shaved and smelled of soap. He was heavenly at close quarters. He had an eager, smiling face and apparently boundless high spirits and this very curly hair which he tried to smarm down as was the habit then. His eyes, I could now see, were dark hazel.

His uncle introduced me and he shook hands. I gazed at him raptly. He asked what I was up to and I told him about collecting National savings and he made a face and said, "Poor you." I thought this showed great perception.

"I don't mind," I said, "Because Miss Eburne gives me horse pictures out of the Tatler. Race horses mostly."

He didn't seem to know how to answer this, and then Mrs Andrews said his bacon was ready so he kindly bought four sixpenny stamps with the rest of his change and went to eat his breakfast.

After that, I knew I had a hero in my life. Most of the

girls at school had Frank Sinatra, a little skinty teen-ager who sang, and up to now I had had James Mason, a film star with a beautiful voice (not singing, just talking). Only one other girl besides me had James Mason. But now I had John Forrest. I did have a few other real ones, horsey boys who I saw at horse shows, one in particular who always won but of course I never spoke to him. I just trailed after him amongst the horse-boxes and goggled at his winning. He became quite famous later and jumped for England but by then I was married.

FOUR

Apart from living for the day when John came home on leave again, I also lived for horse show days, which I had marked in red ink and exclamation marks on the calendar in my bedroom. Horse shows were run in aid of the Red Cross, for fund-raising, as was every entertainment during the war: concerts and bands playing and sports days and Punch and Judy shows, all arranged by councils to keep the spirits up. Holidays at Home they were called, as no one went on proper holidays any more. The horse shows were not very grand but very competitive and well-attended. I had to get to them by train and walk miles, and sometimes I was so excited to be going that when the day came I got asthma so badly I couldn't go. I used to get asthma a lot. I used to cry and the wheeze went and then it was too late to bother going and that made me cry all the harder. I cried a lot because I couldn't have a pony. There was a girl who show-jumped who had three ponies. She jumped them one after the other. I couldn't believe her luck. Three!

However my prancing did not go unnoticed in school and a very kind teacher called Miss Adams who taught us Latin asked me if I would like a pony, as she had one down in her home in Devon who was doing nothing. She would give it to me if my parents agreed. I raced home and hurled this amazing offer at my mother.

"Don't be so ridiculous!" she cried. "Where on earth would we keep it? In the back garden?"

"We can't afford it," said my father.

"What's wrong with the rabbit?" asked my brother.

We had a cat, who later died from a shrapnel wound, the rabbit and a lot of mice, but what were they compared

23

to a pony? I cried a lot more, I stormed up to my bedroom
and screamed abuse at my mother, and cried on and off for
several days, and eventually was forced to tell Miss Adams
that I couldn't accept her kind offer.

"Perhaps one of your friends would like her? And then
you could ride her. Is that possible?"

This hadn't come into my mind.

Annabel wouldn't dream of it, but Biddy . . . she lived
in the country with fields all round her and she hadn't got
her own pony and she had a darling mother who was into
animals, a real countrywoman, and they even had barns and
stables at the bottom of the garden. I could get to Biddy's on
my bicycle in three-quarters of an hour. Biddy was a good
friend but she was terribly bossy and we had great rows. The
idea of her owning my pony was slightly unnerving. But I
put it to her, in desperation, and she put it to her mother,
and her mother agreed. Biddy could have my pony.

"But it's mine too remember," I swore at her. "It's mine
really."

Biddy just laughed, and wheezed. If I had asthma,
my asthma was nothing compared to Biddy's. Biddy was
generally blue and hunched-up and wheezed almost all the
time, but took absolutely no notice of it at all. She laughed
a lot, and coughed and wheezed. Her father had died of
asthma before she was born, but her mother had married
again and her step-father was an officer in the army and
away nearly all the time. Biddy said he hated her, and only
loved her younger brother and sister who were his, but
whether this was true or not I couldn't tell. Anyway her
mother loved her dearly, much more than my mother loved
me, I used to think. She let Biddy have a pony, at least.

They must have been quite rich too as their house was
large and they had a housekeeper called Ali who had been
Biddy's mother's nanny when she was little. She was a lovely
gnarled old woman with a big nose and freckles who did all
the cooking, as Biddy's mother spent all her time in the

greenhouses in their garden. I loved going to their house. They were very kind to me. I don't think they realised how much they were going to see of me when the pony arrived.

She came up from Devon on the train (in a special horse-van, not on a seat). She was called Dolly Grey and was snow-white, only small, and rather fat. She was not, as we quickly found out, what is known in the magazines as a "perfect child's pony". In fact she was a little devil with a mind of her own, so what with my rowing with Biddy as to my rights ---- "It's my turn to ride!" ----- and chasing after her when she had bucked us off, our Sunday afternoons became quite eventful. I used to ride over to Biddy's as soon as Sunday lunch was over. In the winter this meant that my time was quite short, and I nearly always left it too late to complete the journey home before it got dark. There were no street lights and no lights were allowed on the bike and I used to pedal like a maniac watching in despair as the last of a red winter sun sank out of sight behind the hedgerows. After that it was just local knowledge and good luck, but of course waiting for me was the vituperation of my mother. I will say this for my mother, in spite of blowing up with rage like a faulty boiler every time I arrived home in the dark she never stopped me going. She knew how much it meant.

One day when we were riding, me running and Biddy riding --- ("I do all the work looking after her," Biddy used to argue) --- I followed the pony's thick, crossly-twitching white tail down a lane we hadn't been along for some time and found Biddy halted beside a new five-barred gate staring into a large flat field.

"Hey, look at that."

That was a horsey set-up: a row of six new loose-boxes, some barns holding hay and straw, as well as a trade delivery cart with A and G. Mason, Family Butchers, inscribed on the side, and a dear little Hackney carriage as seen in the show-ring. A large and opulent caravan for living in was parked nearby, and an old banger also inscribed A and G. Mason, Family Butchers. Four heads were looking over the loose-box doors and a woman with a fantastic hair-style was filling feed buckets. We stared.

"It's all new. It wasn't here last time I came down here," Biddy said.

It was hardly five minutes from her house.

Dolly whinnied at the horses in the stables and the woman with the hair looked up. She gave a sort of wave. I leaned my arms on the gate. We went on staring. She finished feeding the horses and then came halfway up to the gate and said, "Do you want something?"

Biddy, who was always glib, said, "Can we look at your

horses?"

I wouldn't have dared.

"If you like ," she said.

Up close she wasn't a gorgeous young thing, but a fortyish woman with lipstick and mascara, and the hair, which stood out, peroxided and hard-permed, all round her head. Not the sort of smiling, tanned young woman who featured in my pony books, working in similar circumstances.

We went in the gate and Biddy (of course) gave me Dolly's reins to hold while she looked at the horses. I tried to get close but Dolly was fidgeting and whinnying and tossing about so I had to walk her away, while Biddy was given a personal tour of the whole place. I heard snippets: "This is our show pony Angel . . . . this is my husband's show-jumper, Flash . . . these are the two Hackneys we show" but I was unable to get near enough to see anything. Then they went into the caravan. I heard the woman say, "I've got the photos taken at our last show . . . "

When they had finished and Biddy came back to me I complained bitterly and Biddy said, "Well, she's your pony. You're always wanting your turn, aren't you?" I really hated her.

"If you live near, you could come and help sometimes, if you want," the woman said. "Mucking out and that."

"Oh yes," we glowed.

It was starting to go dark and Biddy knew I had to get back to my trusty bicycle (a sixteen hand liver chestnut hunter called Talisman) to get home so she said we'd come next weekend, and nobly gave me the ride back to her house. As it was going home Dolly bolted back up the lane and I couldn't stop her, and by the time Biddy came wheezing in I had untacked the pony, put her away and was getting on my bike. That was the trouble with Biddy, when I rode I always left her gasping in my wake which made me feel bad.

But she felt the same as me about our amazing luck

in finding a proper stable just down the road, where we would have the privilege of mucking out. The nearest we had got so far to a proper stable was at the coal-yard in her village where they let us have a lift on the coal carts as they went out, sitting amongst the coal bags. On the ground the kindly men reckoned we were in danger: "You don't want to let your little feet near them danged great 'ooves, do you now?" Too true. But the horses were so gorgeous, we loved delivering coal. There was a big stable where I lived where they kept the United Dairy horses but they wouldn't let me in, however long I hung around the gate. The men shooed me away as if I were stray dog, hardly refraining from throwing stones. The glimpses inside were so delicious: two long rows of horses' bottoms almost as far as the eye could see, standing in stalls on either side of a wide corridor. Being milkmen's, they were home by afternoon. I only knew one, Ben, who came down our road, and I knew he was in there somewhere. He knew me, and would have whickered to me if I could have got at him, but I never succeeded.

We told Annabel about our amazing discovery and she said with a shrug, "Oh, the Masons." There was a sneer in her voice.

"They show their hackney in the trade classes, but he never actually delivers meat, only goes to shows. The butcher's cart is just a show cart."

"You mean they aren't really butchers?"

"Oh yes, they are. They've got shops all over. But the showing . . . it's their hobby. The show jumper's quite good, and the pony too, but they can't ride and they're always looking for riders. There's a boy who rides for them but he's not very keen."

Biddy and I digested this information in silence. We both saw the enormous potential of a stable that was short of riders. Just down the road! Amazing. We could ride. We were available. And a boy . . .

Annabel said, "They're rather common."

FIVE

Of course, I might have guessed, Biddy sneaked down to the Mason's stables and inveigled her way in, getting way ahead of me. She went in the evenings and on Saturday mornings while I was queueing for the tiny weekend joint and the vegetables. She met The Boy.

He was called Derek and was no big deal, although love-starved Biddy thought he was. Biddy was truly in love with a farmer called Alan in the Lake District where she spent her summer holidays, but the farmer's mother shooed Biddy away (like me in the United Dairies) because she was too sickly to make a farmer's wife and his mother believed in early discouragement. Alan was to Biddy what my lovely John was to me: a dream to nurture when the brain was otherwise idle. I met him later and it was true, he was lovely. Poor Biddy.

But for now she fell for Derek. I must say, close-up he did have a certain appeal. He was about eighteen, thickset and a bludgeonly rider, but he had a rather handsome face with slightly the look of Clark Gable, and hair like his, dark and a bit long. Mr Mason (the common butcher) was fond of saying, "Wait till you're in the army. You'll get a good close clip when you join up." Derek was a lot more handsome than he was, all the same, Mr Mason looking like one of the "home-raised pigs" advertised on his cart. Biddy decided that Derek was the one for her. He was quite good on the show-jumper but useless on dear delicate little Angel the show hack. I think the Masons thought they could nurture light, skinny little Biddy to show Angel, so they made her welcome. They made me welcome too and handed me a shovel and bucket as soon as I arrived in the yard. Biddy told me in her usual blunt way that they had seen me riding Dolly and said I was useless. This was true as my only riding experience in life was sitting on Dolly for five minutes, getting bucked off or bolted with, or going backwards when I was trying to go forwards, or vice versa, or crying on the side of the road with a fast-vanishing pony disappearing into the distance. So I was never offered a

ride, but I was good at mucking out and cleaning tack and scouring buckets and filling haynets and just hanging around sniffing in the general odour of horse and was actually quite happy.

I enjoyed watching Biddy not getting on very well with Angel.

Angel was a grey about fifteen hands, with a sweet amiable nature, but he was strong. Biddy wasn't strong, poor Biddy, and hadn't the seat power or the leg power to make Angel show off his paces properly. She tried, and I hung over the fence watching, feeling smug, as Mr and Mrs Mason and the boy Derek stood and shouted at her as she went circling round the field. It wasn't the ideal way to produce the mystic fusion of horse and rider, for the three of them between them knew little more than Biddy or myself. I knew the theory, because I devoured every horse book the library had to offer, but the theory of the written word is a far cry from the knowledge that comes with handling and riding horses every day. I just watched as Mr Mason tried to keep his temper and Mrs Mason tried to calm him and Derek bawled useless instructions into the wind. I could see Biddy trying her hardest not to get carted --- actually quite practised at this because of riding Dolly. But not exactly show ring behaviour.

One day when Mr and Mrs Mason had gone out for 'a spin' with the Hackney pony in his butcher's cart Derek decided to give Biddy a lesson. I leaned over the fence to watch as usual as I loved seeing how beautifully the little grey horse moved even with such an inept rider as Biddy. Old know-all Derek instructed her to do this and that and Biddy kept saying, "Yes, Derek," like a real mutt and getting in a terrible muddle, until Derek decided that a few jumps would be just the thing.

"Get his blood up a bit. He's so stuffy . Get him moving."

Biddy looked a bit anxious, as well she might, and Derek pulled out one of the show jumps and set it up. It was quite low.

"Take a canter round now and put him at it," he shouted.

Biddy did as she was told, put Angel at the jump and Angel refused. Biddy shot over his head, hit her head on the heavy wooden wing and lay stunned. Angel kicked up his heels and went racing down the field, his blood well stirred as was Derek's intention, all stuffiness vanished.

Derek said some very common words and shouted at me "Catch that horse!" and he went to see to Biddy. I ran down the field after Angel and caught him without much

31

trouble. I hoped the Masons wouldn't come trotting home at this point, as I am sure they wouldn't have approved of what was going on. But all was well and I took Angel back to his loose-box. As I walked down the field I saw Derek pick Biddy up and carry her in his arms back to the caravan. I knew she weighed hardly anything so it was nothing macho.

I put Angel away in his box and untacked him and put on his elegant sheet. He was so lovely. I laid my head against his warm, lovely-smelling neck and whispered love words to him and he turned his head and nudged me with his sweet rubbery lips. Unlike Dolly, he was so sweet.

Then I thought I had better see what was happening to Biddy, so I walked over to the caravan and went in at at the door. Biddy was lying on the sofa with Derek bending over her in a very undoctorly way and she was far from unconscious, gazing up at him with goo-goo eyes.

"Angel's okay," I said.

One can usually sense when one isn't wanted. Derek straightened up and glowered at me and Biddy gave me a daggers look but I stood my ground. We heard the butcher's cart returning from its spin, and Biddy sat up and said we'd better go.

"Don't tell them," said Derek.

"No, of course not."

On the way home Biddy kept saying, "Oh, it was so lovely in his arms! Like heaven."

"I thought you were unconscious."

"No," said Biddy. "Only pretending."

* * *

Mr and Mrs Mason were East-enders with a sharp eye for anything that might make money. They were making money out of the war, like many sharp, unscrupulous people did. Not that showing made them prize-money, but the

32

wheeler-dealing in smart horses did, which they were in it for. Mr Mason was of an age to be in the army, but he made out that being a butcher was work of national importance and he was exempt. Mrs Mason made quite sure that she was also working in the business and not available for the munitions factory. (Even my mother got roped in for the war effort, being innocent of any Mason-like ploys: she worked in the British restaurants five mornings a week making pies out of carrots for old-age pensioners). They were both quite ugly and never said please or thank-you. Of course, being butchers, they ate like kings and the caravan was always stocked with rarities like butter and sugar and cream cakes so they were well into the black market. (The only extras our family ever got was when we came back from the farm with two eggs or a bit of farm-made butter. My mother would be thrilled, never very good at dividing one fried egg into three parts at breakfast time --- she never ate any.)

Derek worked in the butcher's shop and was waiting for his call-up.

Biddy kept recalling her day in his arms with tedious repetition. She was so boring. I could see that Derek couldn't totally resist her quite obvious devotion, but he never offered to take her out or kiss her or anything. Biddy was actually very pretty, with pink cheeks and blue eyes and lovely blonde hair in two long plaits (we all had plaits, except Annabel who had an expensive perm, not the sort that frizzed) but as she was always overlaid with a sort of blue tinge and wheezed all the time I suppose boys were a bit put off.

Mr Mason tried to turn her into a show-rider for Angel but her strength wasn't up to producing his winning paces. One day, when were riding home with Dolly (Biddy riding and me walking) we were discussing how we could keep in with the Masons if we hadn't anything to offer them except mucking-out and the idea came to us simultaneously.

"Annabel!"

"Of course!"

"And then they'd have to take us to the shows too, because she's our friend!"

"In the lorry. We could ride in the lorry!"

"And be grooms, you know, the sort that stand in the ring to hold things!"

" Annabel would look fantastic on Angel!"

"Oh yes, why ever didn't we think of it before?"

We put this brilliant idea to Annabel at school and she gave us her contemptuous smile and said, "Ride for the Masons?" as if they were the pigs they bred.

"On Angel ---- Angel is divine!" I shouted. "How could you not want to ride Angel?"

"Angel, that little grey in the hack classes?"

"Yes! Yes! He's a real winner but he's got no rider."

"We could get you the ride, we can introduce you --- "

"They are desperate for a rider ---- think of it! You'd win everything."

Annabel was being tempted, we could see. She had seen Angel, because she went to all the shows and we could see that she liked him.

"He's very classy," she said.

"Do you want to meet them and ride him at their place?"

"Where is their place?"

"It's right near mine," Biddy shouted. "You could come to tea!"

Very dubiously Annabel thought she might give it a try. We arranged everything, told the Masons, who were quite excited, and the time of the train that she must catch, so that we could meet her. We actually had a trap for Dolly, which Biddy's mother had unearthed from the cobwebs in one of their garden sheds and we had begged around and made a sort of set of harness that was safe (if not smart) and we quite often drove her down to the local village to do the shopping. She was as good as gold in the trap, better than being ridden. Perhaps that was more her thing. So the great day arrived and we bowled down to the station to meet the train.

Annabel arriving was a bit like the queen dropping in. Dressed in her immaculate riding clothes, tall, beautiful and commanding, she was obviously something a bit new for the gawpers at the station. She was only thirteen, all the same, like us. What was it about Annabel? We never could work it out. We realised at once that the conveyance that was meeting her was hardly up to standard, not with its home-made harness, flaking paint and muddy horse-power, and supposed we should have ordered the taxi but there was only one and in fact it was even more dilapidated than our conveyance. However she climbed in gracefully enough with her contemptuous smile and we drove back home --- cantered actually, as Dolly was hard to stop when going home and we all got the giggles, even Annabel. Dolly wasn't so keen when turned away down towards the lane that led down to the Masons' yard so we arrived at a seemly pace and pulled up at the gate.

Of course, because Dolly was mine, I had to sort her out and put her away in a loosebox while Biddy took Annabel into the caravan and made the introductions. They came out altogether, with Derek, I could see, mightily impressed. I saw at once that our plan was going to misfire as far as Biddy was concerned and I could see that she had already realized the same. It had only taken five minutes.

And of course, when Annabel was up on the little grey horse and they were moving as one, a picture of harmony and elegance such as had never been witnessed in the scruffy Mason homestead before, it was all praise and jubilation. Biddy and I could take the credit but, that apart, we could see we were losers all round. Derek was besotted and we were just for mucking out.

However we shelved our disillusion for now and trotted

back to Biddy's house for tea as promised.

Tea at Biddy's was always a treat as Ali always seemed to manage decent cake even with powdered egg, no fat and a few grains of sugar and Biddy's mother was such a sweetie, always smiling. But with Annabel there we were all a bit on edge and not giggling and messing about as usual. When she departed in the trap with Biddy and I was going out to get on my trusty hunter to cycle home, Biddy's mother said to me,"What a horrible girl! Is she really a friend of yours?"

"Er, yes, I think so." I wasn't really sure, when asked.

Biddy's mother laughed.

"I think there must be nicer girls at school to be friends with."

"Oh yes, there's Anne and Triggy and Biddy and lots. But none of them can ride. Only Annabel. That's why." And this nice woman laughed and said, "Mind how you go now. My regards to your mother." And I fled before the setting sun.

At least Biddy and I got taken to the shows in the lorry. We were usually in the back with the horses while Annabel sat in the front with the Masons and Derek went on his motor-bike, no doubt with petrol siphoned from the butcher's delivery lorry. Then we earned our crust by tacking up, polishing, holding things, filling water buckets, queueing at the secretary's tent, dusting Annabel's boots, finding her gloves, etc. etc. Biddy watched morosely as Derek hung on Annabel's every word. And when she had won her class and was riding around to calm Angel down, (and show off mainly) I noticed that the gorgeous boy who I was in love with, who one day was going to show jump for England, joined her and fell into conversation . And a few shows later she could be seen riding his show-jumper with him, in front of the saddle, the two of them together, he with his arms round her, both of them laughing, while Biddy and I cleared up the dung in the back of the horse-box.

SIX

I lay in bed and listened to the bombers going out. The war had moved on and instead of us having bombs dropped on us we were dropping bombs on them. For the time being we

could sleep in our beds and for now no more beastly nights in the black hole. A lot of the girls at school had come back from Dorset so the numbers were up. Soon they would go back again. People came and went all the time as the war continued. Our school had been bombed, not mortally, but in the winters now we sat in our overcoats and gloves in classrooms without glass in the windows and doors hanging open, askew, chanting our Latin declensions and thirteen times tables, dreading break when we were forced to drink half a pint of freezing milk, unless, like Annabel, we had a note from our doctor to say milk was bad for us. We all had chilblains which itched like mad. I was frozen all the time. At home we had enough coal for one little fire in the evening when my father came home. Roll on summer!

I had a tiny bedroom which faced south and had a lilac tree growing up to the window. My mother believed in early bedtimes and in the summer I used to lie there for ages before I went to sleep. As dusk fell the bombers started to come. They were in perfect formation, three by three, on and on, hour after hour, so that I fell asleep to the soft throbbing of their engines and the smell of the lilac. Perhaps John was up there in his Lancaster? I never found out where he was based. He never talked about what he did. Sometimes when he came home on leave he went playing golf with my father. They had found they were equally matched, both equally bad. He did not always bring a girl.

One weekend I saw his car parked opposite and my heart soared. Lovely National savings, giving me the perfect excuse to knock on his door! They needed a certificate too, having collected a bookful of stamps, and writing out certificates took time.

"Come in, lovey," said Mrs Andrews

Mr Andrews was reading the Sunday Express as usual, Mrs Andrews was cooking the breakfast. John was singing upstairs.

"He's brought his own bacon and eggs, thank goodness. What an appetite! I couldn't feed him otherwise."

I had hardly ever seen a whole fried egg on a plate. We only had one egg a week each. I sat down at the unlaid end of the table and set about sticking a certificate in Mrs

Andrews's book and John came downstairs and sat down opposite his bacon and egg.

Mrs Andrews said to me, "No girl this time. She's thrown him over!"

John laughed. "Peace at last," he said. And to me, "Any good horse pictures lately? Any Tatler ladies driving their hunters down to the shops in the family landau?"

"No. But a lovely one of Straight Deal winning the Derby --- although I wish Nasrullah had won. He should have. And she gave me one of Herringbone winning the Thousand Guineas."

"Herringbone? What a name for a horse!!"

"She was by King Salmon."

I stuck the certificate carefully, very slowly, into Mrs Andrews's book. John was obviously not up in thoroughbred breeding and changed the subject.

"So, anything exciting happened lately?"

"A Jerry came down in a parachute and landed in the tree opposite our school. Some of the girls said they saw him hanging there but they couldn't have because it was in the middle of the night."

"Lucky chap," said John.

"Well not really. They said he was all frizzled and he died when they cut him down. None of us saw him."

I happened to look up and I saw an expression pass over John's face that froze the words on my lips. But it was too late, impossible to take them back --- my stupidity crucified me. I realised my terrible lack of tact the moment the words left my lips, but it was too late to do anything about it. I knew John had baled out and come down by parachute and even if he had landed in the sea and not been 'frizzled' ---- why did I use that terrible, disrespectful word? ---- he hardly wanted to hear of such a tragedy tossed off by a schoolgirl as a bit of exciting news. I could feel a burning flush rising up in my cheeks. But before I could think of anything to say, probably to make it worse, Mr Andrews rustled his Sunday

39

Express and said, "It's amazing they still run the Derby in the middle of a war."

"They say it's to entertain the troops home on leave. Like football and everything that's still going on, " said Mrs Andrews.

"Bloodstock is big business," John said. "The war's not going to last forever."

My terrible blunder all covered up so smoothly that I almost thought it hadn't happened.

"Newmarket is a terrible blasted heath," said Mr Andrews. "Epsom is much nicer.If you want to go racing at all, that is."

He obviously didn't.

"I wouldn't mind a whizz out to Epsom this afternoon," John said. "My new engine still needs running in. Want to come?"

This last question was directed at me. I felt my jaw drop open. I was speechless.

Mrs Andrews said, "She's probably got better things to do, dear."

"No, oh no, I haven't!" I gasped.

"It's terribly draughty in that thing. If you go wrap up well, dear, even if it's lovely and sunny. And John, you must ask her parents. They might not like it."

"Fine, I'll ask them."

Across the road I could see my father's legs sticking out from under his car which was parked outside the garage. This was usual on a Sunday.

"I'll ask him! I'll ask him now! I'm sure he'll say yes," I gabbled.

My heart was pounding as if I'd been running a race. A drive out with my hero! Just wait till I told Anne! I couldn't believe my luck. And after making such a boob! I gathered up my things and flew across the road.

"Daddy! Daddy! Listen --- John says ---- John asked me ---- "

My father thought it very funny.

"Wish he'd asked me! In that thing --- yes, good luck to you. He's got a new engine in it so that'll keep his speed down."

"Cor, I wouldn't mind a ride in that," Peter said. My father's terrible old Ford Popular was not a great wow with Peter. When war broke out my father had had to sell his darling V8 as it ate up too much petrol. Nobody had petrol now, unless they did something special. Hardly any people in our road had a car anyway, so it didn't make much difference. I supposed John siphoned some out of his bomber.

My mother wasn't very keen but gave a grudging permission.

"What's happened to his girl-friend?"

"She's chucked him over," I said in disbelief.

"You'd better wear your winter coat."

So then we had a row over what I should wear, a very common argument. We had so few clothes as they all had to be bought with a very measly supply of coupons --- one winter coat and that was about it for the year, no coupons left for anything else. I was fast growing out of my winter coat and my mother was determined it would be threadbare before we gave it up. I won the row this time, as it was a beautiful day, so met John in the afternoon dressed in the only rig-out I possessed that wasn't school uniform, a green dress which I actually liked and a white cardigan of my mother's. (I wore grey shorts all the time at home but I didn't think these were suitable for the occasion. I had been secretly hoping that John would wear his uniform but of course he didn't. He only wore it coming and going.)

So I drove out with John in his little red MG hardly believing what was happening and we came to Epsom downs and he parked up near the start of the race-course. It was a normal Sunday afternoon with families walking the dog and picnicing and boys flying kites and the view was as beautiful as always with all the woods and hills of Surrey spreading away into the distance as far as the eye could see. We got out and he stood there looking at it, very quiet for once, and sad, I could see. I didn't say anything, but thought for a moment what it was like for him, being here now, and up in the sky in the dark with the shells bursting all round him tomorrow, or the next day, so strange. I walked away, feeling a bit weepy, but then he came after me laughing, and we were standing on the hallowed turf of the race-course where all those famous hooves had pounded through the centuries, at least for the last one and a half.

"The first Derby was in 1780," I said.

"Was there a photo in the Tatler?"

We walked along the course and up the hill towards Tattenham Corner and I told him about the amazing horses: Humorist who won and died of tuberculosis a week later; Hermit who won in a snowstorm (in June); Signorinetta a filly who won at a hundred to one, the love-child of two horses who always whinnied to each other when they met . . .

"A love child?" John was getting confused.

"Yes, the mare was in love with the stallion Chaleureux and her owner who was a dear sentimental old man let them get mated and the result was a Derby winner. Chaleureux never got any winners apart from that one."

I realised this conversation was not going very far with John, so I shut up and we walked on and back through the woods but it was too lovely up there to go home so soon so we sat in the grass and John smoked and I made daisy chains.

I asked him what he did when he wasn't in the RAF but he said he joined the RAF when he left school.

"It seemed a good life to me, flying. The war's made it a bit different, of course."

That seemed to me quite an understatement.

"Do you like it now?"

He did not answer but gave me a funny, sideways smile.

42

"Sometimes," he said. "Coming home."

I didn't ask any more stupid questions and after a bit he said, "What are you going to do?"

"I'm going to be a WAAF."

"The war'll be over by the time you're old enough. You'll have to think of something else."

"An artist then."

"You like painting?"

"Yes, it's my best subject. I paint horses mostly."

He laughed. "I might have guessed."

I told him about Dolly and getting bucked off all the time and about Annabel queening it on Angel and then I thought how stupid it all must seem to him. He was taking it all in, looking at me with his lovely hazel eyes which seemed to smile all the time. I'm not sure how old he was, I think a bit over twenty. He seemed to like listening to me spouting all my rubbish and when we got up to go he said, "It's a pity you're not a bit older."

Afterwards I thought about this and tried to work out exactly what he meant by it. It seemed to me to mean that if I was a bit older I could have been his girl friend. As it was I was just a talkative little schoolgirl.

So I said, "I will be soon."

And he laughed. "Won't we all?"

The afternoon was growing golden and the picnickers were putting their things away.

"I suppose we ought to go home," John said. "I have to get back tonight."

"Tonight!"

"I'm not on leave. Only a couple of days off."

"When's your next leave?"

"Not for a bit yet. I go to Canada after this tour, to instruct for a month or two. Sort of holiday."

I digested this. Canada . . . so far away!

But he wished I was older!

We drove home, quite sedately because of the new

43

engine, and we travelled the same bypass where I cycled so ardently back and forwards from Biddy's, trying to beat the sun as it sank below the horizon.. It was going down now but it was no threat today, just a wonderful glowing finish to a heavenly afternoon.

SEVEN

We were fast growing out of Dolly. She was only eleven and a half hands high, after all. Our dear Latin teacher Miss Adams said she would take her back to Devon in the summer, but how about bringing her to school first so that she could take part in the Latin play? We did a Latin play in the school garden before we broke up, swanning around in diaphanous draperies out of the school's vast collection of mothy theatrical costumes and trying not to get the giggles. We got the giggles with incredible ease.

"Caesar adsum iam forte,
Brutus aderat.
Caesar sic in omnibus,
Brutus in is 'at.'"

This convulsed us at all times. The thought of Dolly in the Latin play was full of delicious possibilities. Was it our idea or Miss Adams'? I think Biddy suggested it. It meant her riding Dolly to school about ten miles all along the bypass and through the trolleybuses up the high street but, wheezing valiantly, she arrived safely at milk time and we all trailed out to welcome her. She tied the pony up in the bicycle shed. Dolly was to stay for a rehearsal in the afternoon and then go out to be lodged in the local riding school for the night. But before this happened Dolly kicked the bicycle shed to bits and was found still tied to the pole with her feet through a pile of broken bicycles, covered in sheets of corrugated iron off the roof. With cries of horror we extricated her and examined her for injury, during which time our headmistress sailed out (she was a very large lady) and gave us all a good dressing down, even poor Miss Adams who stood trying to look as if she had nothing to do with it.

Dolly's contribution to the play was not a success either. It took place in the beautiful, overgrown garden behind the school, not in the school hall. Groomed and bathed and looking clean but hardly elegant Dolly was ridden on stage by the hero, whereupon she lifted her tail and dumped a great steaming pile of poo in the middle of the climactic speech, convulsing the audience of parents who were sitting politely, not understanding a word, waiting for this tedious exhibition to end. They got the giggles as badly as the rest of us who were rolling abut helplessly behind the trees, waiting for the final bow. My father loved it.

Then Dolly was sent back to Devon. We had to put her on the train and luckily Annabel came over to help as we had to go on our bikes, leading her, miles to the mainline station where a horse wagon was waiting in a siding. Some nice men helped us to box her and we left her munching away at a large haynet, waiting to be hooked up to the next train. It was very sad saying goodbye. Biddy and I cried. Annabel didn't.

We were going to miss Dolly. But I would still cycle over to Biddy's and quite often stay the night, which I loved. At Christmas they were going to have a big party. Alan and his family were coming down from the Lake District and Biddy was so excited on the day that she got the wheezes really badly. We went round in the afternoon building up fires in the old grates which were going to take their whole coal ration for a month at least. Their house had large, old-fashioned rooms which were wonderful for playing Sardines and having Charades and dancing and party was marvellous. It was true that Alan was lovely, just as Biddy said. He was a large , muscular young man with the quiet demeanour of some one used to working with animals, a slow sweet smile and very green eyes.

Annabel came.

Why did Biddy invite her? I had to, she said afterwards, which I suppose was true. But Alan was hypnotized by her, of course, following her every move as she twirled around in her gorgeous (black market) dress, favouring him with her derisive, come-on smile. Even when he was dancing with Biddy (very slowly, for her breathing) he was looking over her shoulder, searching for Annabel. They could not help themselves, these country boys, seeing the exoticism that Annabel expressed in the way she looked at them. I suppose she couldn't help it herself.

I had been invited to stay the night. When everyone had gone home we got undressed and into our nighties in front of the dying embers of the fire. Ali brought in a steaming bowl of Friar's Balsam for Biddy to breathe and her mother brushed out her lovely blonde hair and replaited it, slowly and gently. It must have been hard for her to see Biddy's plight and not be able to do anything about it, but she was so calm and loving. I watched her as the firelight played on her sad face, wishing she was my mother. My mother never brushed out my hair; I went to bed with it as it was and did it myself in the morning. In our house it was always brisk; "Hurry up now, quick sharp. Be quick!" But here we were tucked up with old hot water bottles (we only had one stone one at home, the old rubber ones perished and now unobtainable) and I heard Biddy crying, but what could I do about it? I just vowed I would never let Annabel meet my dear John.

I did go to Annabel's house occasionally and met the ghastly father. Funnily enough, although he was something to the king and had offices and myriads of bowing and scraping flunkies in St James' palace, he did show us the best way to slide downstairs on a tea-tray without hitting the priceless vase that stood in the hall at the bottom. Annabel had brothers who were in the navy and army with lots of gold braid and medals and things but I never met them. Annabel was 'the baby' and could do no wrong. Her mother was old and arthritic and was rarely seen out of her rooms. The house was enormous and you met maids and men in nice suits who stood to one side to let you come by. My mother was all ears when I told her about it.

"Fancy," she said. "Fancy that!"

But I must say I felt more at home when I went to the farm at weekends, more often now that were was no pony at Biddy's. There were horses at the farm who did all the work --- Molly and Punch and Boxer and Ben, great gentle things who did everything just by word of mouth. Peter had always gone to the farm at weekends when he wasn't playing his euphonium or tinkering in the garage with my father. The farmer's son Fred was in the same class at school and his best friend and they worked together on the farm, hedging and ditching in the winter or cutting out turnips from the great clamps on the side of the fields, harvesting in summer. Peter had made himself so useful that Freddie's father was always pleased to see him even when he was trailing his sister. I was given the same jobs, tending the bonfire when they were laying a hedgerow (Peter was really good at cutting and laying), fetching a tool they had forgotten from the farm about half a mile away, pitch-forking reeking manure over the fields, pitch-forking hay in the summer.

I never learned to milk though and nor did Peter. Freddie and his father did the milking, Freddie before he came to school, and again when he got home. Freddie liked me and once when we were sitting on a cart full of manure going out to a distant field he told me what lovely little hands I had. He advanced his own great dung-smeared mitt to cradle one of mine but his father who was following in a cart behind bellowed at him and he jumped back. That was the nearest he ever got to courting. Once Peter and I stayed the night and when we went to bed Freddie's mother led us up the stairs with a candle and put it on the window-sill. I was enchanted.

Of course we never got paid. We were all expected to work for the war effort and the older girls at school used to get shunted off to farms to work in the summer holidays. It wasn't compulsory but lots went and tales came back of working with delectable young German prisoners. Apparently when you were all stooking corn in the hot sun for eight hours a day it didn't much matter which side you were on. A lot of German prisoners worked on farms but Freddie's father refused to take them. I really looked forward to being old enough to go farming with the school. It was said to be great larks, camping out, but the work was killing.

Peter was soon to leave school and he was to be apprenticed to a big engineering firm in Bedford, arranged by my father, to study for his mechanical engineering degree. So that he could come home at weekends my parents bought him a motor-bike, a handsome beast called an Ariel Red Hunter. Everyone came to admire it. My father rode it, and I was allowed to travel to the farm on the pillion to show it off. My mother knew we rode nearly all back lanes to the farm, so she said, "Just go slowly, Peter. Be careful." Of course he drove it straight out to the bypass and said to me, "Let's see how fast she'll go."

It was terrific. He got it to over eighty and we went miles in no time at all, halfway to Portsmouth, and then on the way home we had to call in the farm and try and get in the right frame of mind to go home, pretending it had been boring.

It seemed our games were coming to an end as, with Peter departed and no Dolly to ride and school getting ever more earnest, I realised I was growing up. I hope John would notice when he came back from Canada. Mrs Andrews remarked on it when I went for the National Savings.

"You're quite a young lady now. How time passes! The war will be over by the time you're ready to leave school."

"But I want to be a Waaf!"

"I don't suppose they'll want you, dear, not by then. Please God John will come through safely. He's been so lucky so far. When he comes back he's moving on to one of those American bombers --- enormous things. Flying Fortresses or some name like that."

"When's he coming back?"

"In three months time. It gives them a rest, for their nerves."

"Why can't the Americans fly them?"

"They do, dear. So many bombers going out now, Americans and all. It can't last much longer, not when D day comes."

We were all waiting for D day, the day we moved out across the Channel and landed all our troops in France to take back the occupied countries. We knew we were winning now, listening to the news every night and hearing how we were advancing through Italy and the Russians were advancing into Eastern Germany and the bombers were bombing the Ruhr and Hamburg, Cologne, Frankfurt, Dortmund, Dusseldorf, Essen, Stuttgart . . . the names were as familiar to us as Blackpool, Birmingham and Guildford. We listened to all this on the wireless. The names of the German cities rolled off our tongues, but I do not think we often stopped to think where they were or what it meant, only when it said how many of our bombers 'failed to return'. People said these figures were 'massaged', made less than they really were. But how were we to know? Just as they said how many German fighter planes were shot down, far more than was true, feel-good figures.

I just thought of John in his bomber with the Messerschidts coming at him, guns blazing, and all the while the plane keeping to its steady course as the bomb doors were opened and the target was illuminated below by the flare dropped by the path-finders. To keep straight, unyielding, patient, until the bombs were released . . . what incredible cool! The shellfire coming up from below becoming more and more accurate as the target got nearer because the gunners could estimate exactly the bomber's course . . . it did not bear thinking about. As I grew up, so my childish excitement at being part of the war changed into an understanding of the real horrors of it.

The day in June when D day, so long anticipated, actually happened was marked in school by a special assembly in the hall to listen to the news on the crackling radio set up rather inefficiently on the stage, and then we had prayers and were all sent home for the rest of the day. It was terribly solemn and terribly exciting. We all thought then that the war would be over in no time.

EIGHT

It was very strange. Ten days after D day the air raid siren went in the evening and the All Clear didn't sound until after breakfast the following morning. I went to school after the All Clear, nice and late, but while I was waiting on the station platform the siren went again. Nobody knew what was going on. We hadn't had any raids for some time now.

When I got to school we had to go in the shelters all day because there was no All Clear. It was very squashy as most the girls who had been evacuated had come back and the school was quite full and normal again. The gossip was that all this was because of Hitler's new secret weapon, the flying bomb. It had no pilot and came across from the enemy coast all on its own, aimed in the general direction of London. When its power ran out it fell to earth wherever it happened to be. We thought this was very funny and jeered. Hitler's last throw --- he was desperate.

We didn't jeer for long.

"I saw one!" shouted Peter, triumphant, home from school on his bike.

"What's it like?"

"It's just a bomb flying through the air with an engine mounted on top and flames coming out behind. It makes a terrific racket."

No sooner had the words left his mouth than a terrific racket started approaching very fast and my mother screamed, "Get in the shelter! Get in the shelter!" Of course we wouldn't, so anxious to see this amazing thing. We dawdled across the lawn and saw it as it shot over, very low, just as Peter had described it. Then just as it was disappearing in the direction of the sewage works the engine cut out and there was a complete silence. Peter and I froze, our mouths dropped open. The silence seemed to last for ever, until there came an enormous explosion and the earth shook beneath our feet.

Peter and I gaped at each other. This was something quite different. No warning, distant approach of bombers, not even the quite slow, almost musical whistle of dropping bombs, but such quick sharp action and fury that one could not hope to prepare for it.

Thinking the war was shortly going to end and we at home were now quite safe, everyone was as shocked as probably Hitler had hoped. The air raid sirens could not cope with these indiscriminate visitations and seemed to go on and off at random so that in the end there was no point taking any notice of them. All the girls who had filtered back to school promptly disappeared again. Biddy went up to dear Alan in the Lake District; Anne, in spite of God's will, went to Cornwall, Annabel to Devon and I . . . "As soon as your exams are over you can go up to Auntie Hilda in Birmingham."

My father was away working all this time. He had ordered a Morrison shelter, which was a great iron table that the council workers brought and erected indoors. It had heavy wire netting all round it and you lay squashed in together at night and tried to go to sleep. The idea was that if the house fell down on top of you you were safe under the table. I must say that it wasn't enough to inspire confidence when one lay listening to the terrible racket of the flying bomb overhead and its engine cut out. The ensuing seconds before the big bang were truly frightening. It was the only time during the whole war that I was seriously frightened. The windows of our house were blown in; our school was hit and badly damaged (at night fortunately) and a lot of houses in our unfortunate suburb were blown to bits along with their inhabitants.

Peter was doing his General Certificate exams all through this and went to school every day on his bike --- not the motor-bike. In September he was departing for Bedford and I couldn't imagine life without him, even if we did still fight like wild cats. I was to go to Birmingham, dear John was in Canada: it seemed like partings all round. Peter refused to come to Birmingham. He was going to spend all his holiday on the farm. He half wanted to be a farmer, not an engineer, but we didn't have a farm so the opportunity wasn't there. Maybe Freddie wanted to be an engineer: who knows? They both had new girl friends whom they met at the Young Farmers, two good friends who they later married, one each. Both these girls lived farther out in the country so didn't have doodlebug trouble. These flying bombs were called doodlebugs: I'm not sure where this word came from but its sneering tone was something of a comfort and was universally used.

When the time came I was mightily relieved to go to Birmingham. My only regret was that dear John was due home from Canada shortly and if he went straight back to bombing again I wouldn't see him for ages. Our bombers were now going out in daylight as well as at night time and doing terrible damage if one believed what it said on the wireless. It was obvious by now that the war was won, and the pressure was on to make Hitler capitulate. But of course he wouldn't, and never did, so that thousands and thousands of people, both military and civilian, went on getting killed right up to the time he committed suicide. At home, of course, it was our own skins we were worried about. The silent sky over my Auntie Hilda's house was bliss.

Auntie Hilda, a staid old thing, lived outside Birmingham in a leafy suburb. Her daughter, my cousin, was a WAAF, but I never saw her while I was there.

It didn't matter, for in no time at all I was part of a gang who lived in the road. They were mostly boys but with one heavenly horsey girl called June. June was slightly older than me, very beautiful and cool, and rode at a stable with lots of ponies that all needed exercising. We rode every day and went on larks with the boys every evening. I was in paradise. I thought June was the most gorgeous creature who had ever come my way and was amazed when my auntie said slyly, "I think Ronald's in love with you."

"Ronald!"

Ronald was June's younger brother. I could hardly tell him I was in love with his sister, so suffered him taking me to the pictures to see "Dangerous Moonlight", an incredibly sad film which made me cry my eyes out. But as Ronald insisted on holding my hand I couldn't get at my handkerchief and had to sit hiccuping with tears running down my cheeks. I wasn't aware of the protocol of holding hands in the cinema and thought it would be rude to pull my hand away to blow my nose. Ronald had no intention of releasing me and appeared not to notice my plight. I wasn't impressed, apart from the realization that this was my first 'date', a milestone of a sort, the kind of thing I would enjoy spilling into Anne's sympathetic ear. She was writing to me about all the boys she was meeting in Cornwall, and Biddy was penning paeans of delight about milking cows with Alan, with his hands on hers to show her how, but I felt I could hardly write back to say that I had fallen in love with a girl, even if her brother fancied me.

But after a month school beckoned once more and the doodlebugs had dwindled somewhat so I went home. Peter was off to Bedford to start working for his living but --- joy of joys --- John was back from Canada and at home awaiting a posting to a new bomber base. I ran up the road on Sunday morning to collect my National Savings and was pounding on the door of Mr Andrews' house at nine thirty.

It was a beautiful late summer day. There was the sound of lawn mowers being pushed across the handkerchief lawns, the usual spanner noises coming out of our garage and my father's voice singing ("Cherry Ripe, cherry ripe, ripe I- I -I cry") from underneath the car and the crackle of Peter's Red Hunter as he tuned it ready for Bedford. My mother was cooking the Sunday joint (such as it was) and making lemon meringue pie (without lemon or eggs, a very clever achievement) and as I waited on the Andrews' doorstep I felt as if I had been away a year, not a mere month. It was the first time I had ever left home, except for summer holidays before the war, and the odd night at Biddy's or Anne's. I thought of John visiting Germany every night; how strange!

He had grown a moustache. It was horrid. But the same lovely eyes smiled at me over the toast and marmalade and he asked me all about my adventures. I didn't tell him I had temporarily fallen in love with a girl.

"How was Canada?"

"Hard work. I didn't see much of it, hardly ever off the base."

"Good food though," said Mrs Andrews. "You should see what he's brought back! You can take some butter for your mother when you go."

"Oh, lovely! She'll be pleased. She can't keep up with Peter, she says."

"No, well, growing boys getting the same ration as a toddler is not very clever, is it? She must be at her wit's end. John always brings stuff, but this time . . . ! Look, look at this --- "

It was a banana, rather blackened with travel across the Atlantic, but still eatable. She gave it me, and then an orange!

"And one for Peter."

I couldn't believe it.

"How wonderful!"

"So what do you think of our young lady, John? She's growing up fast, isn't she? We missed her while she was away. And Peter's off too." She chuntered on, fishing in her handbag for her money, rootling along the mantelpiece for her savings book. John was looking at me in a contemplative way. I wondered if he too thought I was older now, as once he had wished. Was I catching up? But he too, somehow, looked older as well. He had fine, sad lines round his eyes and a way of, somehow, switching off in the middle of general conversation, as if he had more important things to think about.

"Are you home for long?" I asked him.

"I don't know. I doubt it. We're getting these American crates --- "

"Flying Fortresses," I butted in, excitedly. Peter and I knew all about them. The Americans, and their machinery, were now here in force and some of the girls in our class had American boy-friends. Or said they did. One of them produced a pair of nylon stockings to prove it. Nylons were supposed to be very desirable, but I was still in ankle socks. The American soldiers were certainly very desirable, so forthcoming and friendly, offering packets of gum as well as nylons, and all dressed like officers even when they weren't, in immaculate, tight-fitting uniforms of expensive cloth. There weren't any around where I lived but the clever girls at school knew where to find them. I hadn't met one yet.

"Do you want to come out this afternoon?" John asked me. "It's too nice to stay in. We could go down to the river and get a boat."

"Oh yes! That would be lovely!"

We used to go on the river (the Thames) quite often as a family, my father and Peter rowing and my mother and I sitting in the back steering. You had a rope from the rudder over your shoulder, one each, and pulled it to go left and right. My mother and I used to go in great loops, not entirely by mistake, and my father used to get furious and my mother and I would get the giggles. I loved the elegant skiffs with their golden velvet cushions and cane-backs

58

seats. It was a very Sunday afternoon thing to do.

I rushed home with the butter and oranges and shouted that I was going to go rowing with John and Peter taunted me and said, "He's much too old for you! You can tell ---- he's going bald! His hair is receding --- "

I went at him hammer and tongs and he got hold of me by the wrists and held me at arm's length, laughing and jeering, so I kicked out with my feet and he started giving me Chinese burns, so I screamed and my mother came rushing out (this was going on in the garage) and told us to shut up, what would the neighbours think?

"They think she's too young to go out with an old ---- "

I kicked him again and my father put his head out from under the car and said, "Tell him when you get back, if there's time for a round of golf, I'll be ready."

So after dinner John called for me and we went down to the river and hired a skiff. I settled in the golden cushions with both ropes to myself (which made steering much easier than when there were two of you doing it) and John started to row up river against the current and, as he faced me, I could recline and feast myself on his lovely figure. He was his usual joky self now, laughing and making me laugh, and I was filled with a happiness I had never experienced before, watching John with the golden afternoon sun making a halo round his head, the water glinting under the oars, the ducks hopeful for a bit of sandwich paddling in our wake. The banks were lined with trees and there were people cycling along the towpath and out walking their dogs, children running and shouting, lots of other boats and sailing dinghies drifting about.

The war seemed so far away, and yet there could easily be a doodlebug if we were unlucky; they had not entirely disappeared. And I knew when I went to bed I would hear the drone of the bombers going out, as always. It never went away these days. John too would hear them tonight. When I looked at him now, rowing in his shirt sleeves, recounting some ridiculous joke he had heard, laughing, teasing me, I found it hard to reconcile his presence here on the tranquil Thames in the sunshine with his immediate future in one of those bombers in the black sky amongst the shellfire, killing. It made no sort of sense. How could his brain come to terms with it? Habit, I presumed, and the inevitability of it, the impossibility of making it any different. For myself, I could not get my head round it. I put it away from my thoughts and laughed too. He got tired of rowing and told me to turn into the bank to give him a rest.

"We can tie up under those willows for ten minutes. You can tell me what boys you've been seeing while I've been away."

Telling him about Ronald wouldn't take long.

There were other skiffs laid along the bank, their occupants picnicking or snogging or dangling their feet in the water, and John made for a gap. With my excellent steering we reached it just before another skiff that was making for the same gap, and John nipped in neatly, shipped his oars and stood up to grab the painter from the bows. As he did so the other skiff hit us amidships with a great crash and shouts of, "I say, I say, old chap! Awfully sorry!"

John was nearly pitched overboard but he retrieved his balance and caught hold of a willow branch to pull us in.

"Don't worry about it!" he called across. "Not our boats!"

The other rower was a young man in immaculate casual dress, slightly long-haired and under-chinned, a complete buffoon as he tried to back-paddle, losing one oar in the process.

"Oh, Monty, don't be such a fool," said a cool, familiar voice from the cushions in the stern, and I turned to see to my horror Annabel lolling in the back seat.

Her eyes were so fixated on John that she didn't notice me for some moments. When she did her jaw dropped.

"Whatever are you doing here?"

What was I supposed to answer to that? While poor Monty made a terrible hash of retrieving his lost oar and nearly falling overboard, she put out her arm and got hold of our skiff and said to John, "Perhaps we could come alongside?"

Oh, that honied voice, those come-on eyes, that cheek! She was gazing right into his face and I saw a bemused look come into his eyes. He was ready to be hooked, like them all, another poor fish.

I gave her boat a great shove-off with my foot that nearly tipped it over and snapped, "No, you can't! There's plenty of room farther along. Go and find your own place."

Annabel gave me an amused look, knowing exactly what I was thinking, and --- thank goodness --- told Monty to back off.

"I'll see you at school," was her parting shot, obviously imagining that John didn't know I was only a school girl.

Monty splashed away, John tied up our boat and then came and sat beside me on the back seat and pulled out a packet of cigarettes.

"A friend of yours?" he queried. "That's no way to treat your friends." But he was laughing.

"I hate her," I muttered. " She's in my class. She's horrible."

"She's very --- " He paused.

I waited.

"Predatory, I should say. Not your sort, I would have said."

I made a mental note to look up predatory in the dictionary when I got home. I associated it with wolves, somehow. Predatory animals.

"We do quite a lot together because she's horsey. She's a very good rider."

He didn't know that I wasn't, that I was only there for the mucking out. He must have recognized the look she gave him. I supposed he was used to it, the come-on looks from girls.

Obviously he wasn't feeling predatory for he lay back in the cushions and smoked his cigarette and made no move to hold my hand like Ronald, or kiss me, which seemed to be what all the other occupants of our neighbouring skiffs were doing. I knew I was just his friend, still too young, although slowly getting there. I suppose I was a novelty after the tarty WAAFs he used to bring home and I guessed he kissed them passionately. But not me. Yet he never made me feel that he found me wanting, quite the opposite. I suppose he found me restful, undemanding, when obviously all the other part of his life wasn't.

When we got home he went off again in my father's car to play a round of golf and later in the evening when they got back we all played cards. It was a very joky evening and we stayed up quite late, which was very unusual for my mother to allow. I thought it must be the butter that had cheered her up. I guessed she was trying not to think of Peter leaving home the next week and I was trying not to think of John going.

When he went home I went out into the garden with him. It was a beautiful night but already the first bombers were droning in the sky. He stood at the gate, silent, listening, his hands in his pockets. I tried to think what he was thinking but it made me feel like crying. Then he turned to me, smiled, and kissed me very gently on the cheek, and said, "Till my next leave then. Be good."

Then he was gone.

NINE

John went back the next day, very early. I don't know what alerted me, but I got out of bed and went to the front window and saw him come out of the house with his aunt and uncle. He was in uniform and carrying his bag which he dropped in the passenger seat of the car. Then he turned and embraced his aunt. I could see she was crying. He tried to cheer her up, I could see, but not with much success, so he gave up and shook hands with his uncle, gave his aunt a last kiss and drove away. Did he look across at my house in parting? I don't think so. I saw Mr Andrews put his arm round his wife's shoulders and they went indoors, looking older that usual.

When I called on them the following Sunday Mrs Andrews was her usual cheerful self.

I asked if she had heard from John and she said, "Yes, dear. He's flying one of those American planes now. He says they're nicer than Lancasters."

"What do you mean, nicer?" Mr Andrews growled from behind his Sunday paper. "How can a bomber be nice, or nicer?"

"That's what he said."

"I don't see anything nice about them."

"You're not flying one, dear. I'm only repeating what he said. Five shillings, lovey, and I want a new book. This one's full."

"When will he be home again?"

"Well, he's just started a new tour so I suppose when he gets to the end of it." And then to my horror her eyes filled with tears and she said, "He's gone on so long and now the war is nearly finished I just dread that he might not come through. After all this time . . . he's been so lucky . . "

Mr Andrews rustled his paper and said, "Come, come, he's had his share of mishaps. Crash-landed once, baled out into the sea --- he was lucky there, wasn't he, to get picked up? His fair share, I'd say. Of course, he'll come through. It's nearly over now."

"I never used to worry quite so much. I suppose it's because we know it must be nearly over, our troops advancing so quickly and everything." She blew her nose and smiled at me."I'm so sorry, dear. I didn't mean to sniffle.. It's just what you read in the papers , and when it says on the radio every day how many bombers missing from the night before . . . my blood runs cold, I can't help thinking it might be John. I can't help myself."

She had never been like this before. What she was saying made my blood run cold too. I heard these figures on the radio every day as well, but up to now they had only been figures. It was true we saw the bombers coming home early in the morning, no longer in formation but in ones and twos, and sometimes you could see some of them were damaged, with bits hanging off them and an engine cut out or even trailing smoke, but they were the survivors and I always saw them with a feeling of pride and gratitude without thinking of the ones who had not managed to get back.

* * *

Annabel had interrogated me about my partner in the skiff and I had told her he was a flight-lieutenant in the RAF, a bomber pilot, and although she tried not to show it I could tell she was impressed. Most of the girls had dribbled back to school since the doodlebugs fizzled out (the troops had advanced far enough to capture their launching bases) but school was a miserable place as summer gave way to autumn.

It had been hit in the holidays and none of our classrooms had windows any more and few even had doors. We had had to spend the first few days sweeping and cleaning and gathering up all the glass and now the builders were in boarding everything up. There was dust everywhere. The boilers were not on and it was freezing. Perhaps to cheer us up we upper forms were offered Ballroom Dancing as an extra which was quite a laugh. I danced with Annabel --- she was the man, of course --- and we tripped about counting our quick quick slow, quick quick slow, or our one two three, one two three, and getting the giggles when we were taught how to be presented at court, how to curtsey deeply without falling over and how to walk between two lines of people bowing in turn to either side. I thought this was terrific. I showed Peter when he came home, how to walk bowing to either side when presented at court.

"So when's that going to happen?"

"I can't see that ever starting up again, somehow," my mother said. "Not after all this."

Nor could I. It was so funny, for a start, and so completely irrelevant. Even if it did, I knew I was not the right sort of person. Annabel was, of course. She would be there, bowing to left and right with her come-hither eyes searching for talent.

"Is that all you learn at school?" Peter asked derisively.

"No. It's extra for fun. It's part of ballroom dancing. We've been told we might have a dance at school at Christmas, with boys."

"Blimey! Real boys?"

"We can take one and if we haven't got anybody they're going to invite the boys from the Grammar School so there'll be plenty."

"They won't come," Peter said. "Not if they've got any sense."

My secret dream was that John would be home and I could take him. A dance at a girls' school . . . he'd probably rather go on a bombing mission. But meanwhile we learned how not to tread on the boy's feet nor be trodden on ourselves. We were told it was always the girl's fault if this happened. (I disputed this later).

Later in the term we were asked if we would like to join a class on Saturday mornings, with boys. Annabel could see that she needed this, having been a boy for so long and not having learned to dance backwards, so she prevailed upon me to sign up for it. I was quite excited at the thought and my mother agreed. She thought it was a hopeful sign in my development, exchanging ponies for boys.

I was very nervous the first morning but I could see that the boys were even more so. On the whole they were a pasty-faced lot --- one might have expected it after all ---- but there were one or two Hooray Henry sorts whose mothers obviously thought it was an important part of their upbringing to learn not to tread on the girls' feet. The nicest was called Colin . He wasn't a show-off like some (once their nervousness had worn off) but made quite interesting conversation as we quick quick slowed fast down the length of the hall. He knew about the favourite for next year's Derby (Dante) and said he'd made 'a packet' on Ocean Swell last year at six to one, and I told him that when the Derby came back to Epsom I was definitely going to go. It would be my last year of school and I had already worked out that if I went to school on my bike, which I quite often did in the summer, I could skive off school at lunchtime, cycle to Epsom, watch the Derby and cycle home again for a late tea with no questions asked. Epsom was free, unlike Newmarket. Anyone could go.

I really got to look forward to Saturdays and my dancing with Colin. Of course we had to mix up and dance with all the boys and one day in one of these change-abouts Colin got Annabel. I think she manoeuvred it. I got her awful Monty who talked about cricket and rugby and trod all over me. "Awfully sorry," he kept saying, just as when he'd hit us broadside on with his skiff. I was watching Colin and Annabel over Monty's shoulder and could see Annabel at work inveigling Colin ---- my Colin. It was such a familiar act to me now, the way she looked at them in a sort of challenging, almost scornful way, smiling, letting them chatter on, then saying something in a soft, low voice so that they had to bend close to hear her, and she would smile again with her sideways come-on look, her long eyelashes fluttering . . . like a film star. I could see Colin being hooked, just like all the others. When I got him back he asked me who my friend was, what was her name?

"Gertrude Higginbottom," I said crossly.

It was all spoilt. There were only two lessons left and I didn't dance with Colin again. He danced with Annabel.

* * *

It was our exams next summer, the General Certificate, so we were working very hard and it was difficult with the school being so wrecked and freezing and the builders crashing about everywhere and I think the Christmas dance was a sort of present to us to cheer us up. The school had never done this before. I think the staff were very nervous. It was lucky they didn't know that quite a few girls were planning to bring GIs, which was what American soldiers were called; we made quite sure they didn't find out.

"I thought it was only the Grammar school boys," I said.

"You can bring your own boy. Nobody said he had to be a grammar school boy, did they? You could bring your brother, why don't you?"

I had already noticed that girls liked Peter. He was quite good-looking and forthcoming, funny, not a dope. But of course I wouldn't bring him. He wouldn't come for a start.

67

I asked Anne who she was bringing.

"A boy from church called Martin. He's very obliging. He can't dance though."

It was a matter of honour, I suppose, to produce a boy, to show that you had one. I knew I could take a boy who lived up the road, an amiable Grammar school boy who was always happy to come to anything if needed. He was one of Peter's childhood gang and we had all gone birds-nesting and fishing in the stream together when we were little.

Anne said, "You could bring John if he's home on leave."

I had already thought of that but not seriously.

"To a girls' school? He wouldn't come."

"There's lots of GIs coming. Joy asked hers and he thinks it's a great lark and is bringing his pals."

"Blimey!"

I thought of our poor deluded staff who were nearly all past retiring age providing lemonade and buns for nice boys from the Grammar school. Then I thought, if John knew lots of GIs were coming he might be tempted. I knew he mixed quite a lot with the American air force and his bomber was American, after all. They could talk about it. But it was very unlikely he would be home on the right date. And then, dare I ask him? The thought of it made me feel quite funny.

I asked my mother.

"Do you think ---- ?"

She said, "Well, if he's home and he's not got one of his WAAFs with him he might find it quite entertaining." She was very non-committal. "I don't know what on earth you're going to wear. We've no coupons left and you've grown out of your only decent dress."

Thank goodness, I thought. It had smocking over the front, like a baby's, and had been made as a labour of love by the woman next door out of some pre-war shantung that had been lingering in her airing cupboard for half a century. I had hated it like poison from day one.

"Anne might have something. Or there's my green thing."

Annabel got things from her cousins who got things on the black market and would no doubt look stunning, but I wouldn't stoop to borrowing from her. I was still happiest in my grey shorts and Aertex shirts, and otherwise it was school uniform, so I didn't often want proper clothes. I really only had my green dress which I loved, but it was true it was getting tight and short. My plaits were long gone but my hair didn't curl much so I had to put it in curlers every night which was a terrible bore. Posh girls got perms but they were very expensive. My mother tried one but it came out in a great frizz and she was stuck with it until it was long enough to cut off. Peter and I rolled about laughing when we saw it and even she saw the funny side after she had stopped crying. Annabel had a perm but hers didn't frizz. It wouldn't dare. She looked at least twenty when she was done up. I didn't care very much about what I was going to wear as I didn't think John would be home.

"You're much too young to go out with him. Of course, he's not serious, or I would be worried. He's bored when he's at home, poor boy. There's no girls here the right age for him."

I didn't tell her he was waiting for me to age. By the time I had, I always supposed he would have found somebody else. But the way he had said it had given me hope, for it had seemed quite serious. Or was it my imagination? Just a joke? Joy's GI had asked her to marry him and, like me, she was only fifteen.

"He's going to take me home as soon as the war's over."

"Where's home?"

"Wyoming. He's a cowboy."

I found it very hard to get my head round this. We knew all about cowboys because of seeing them in films but Joy didn't know one end of a horse from another and still less about Wyoming. We knew where it was because of our geography lessons but it wasn't anywhere near New York or San Francisco or any normal civilisation. For a girl brought up on the edge of London I could see this might be daunting, but Joy didn't seem to think so.

"What does your mother think?"

"She thinks he's lovely. They're all coming to stay."

"Blimey."

I wasn't sure if John were to come he would have much in common with a cowboy from Wyoming.

"What does he do now?"

"He drives a tank. He's waiting to go to Germany."

I realized I would be much happier if I could find out if John was likely to be home or not, because if he wasn't I could stop worrying and just ask Peter's bird-nesting friend up the road. I was sure he would oblige, because all his friends would be there, the job lot of grammar school boys. I asked Mrs Andrews next Sunday.

"A dance at school? How lovely! My, how you're growing up! I scarcely recognise you these days."

"I wondered if John might come, if he's home."

She would never know what an effort it took me to

deliver these words.

"Well, why not? He doesn't seem to bring those WAAFs home any more. I often think it's really boring for him here, but of course, he needs the rest when he gets time off, so I suppose it suits him. A dance at your school would be quite a novelty, I daresay. Not like the sort he usually goes to."

"What sort does he usually go to?"

"Well, you know, near the aerodrome, they have dances in the village halls and the girls come from all around. Very rowdy. The nights they don't fly --- for the weather, or if they're laid off for a few days for some reason. They go a bit wild when they're off duty I believe."

I had never thought of John in this light, but of course it made sense. I was only familiar with a small slice of John, I knew that. I knew nothing of his working life, his friends, his ambitions. He never talked about his past or his future. If he were to introduce me to his bombing comrades I wouldn't have a word to say. I would die. It completely mystified me how Joy could live it up with a crowd of GIs, cowboys from Wyoming. What was I missing, I wondered? I realised suddenly how pathetic I was, asking him to come a school dance with lemonade and buns.

But Mrs Andrews said, "I'm sure he'll come with you if he's home. I'll try and find out when his next leave is. I'll tell him he's got a date."

"Oh, don't do that! Please!"

She laughed. "I think he's very fond of you."

I nursed this sentence from then on: it nestled in my brain, glowing. Whenever I recalled it a great happiness took hold of me, just as it had once when I used to mark off the days to the next horse show. Only better. I told Anne. She was totally sympathetic.

"It would be fantastic! Lucky you. Martin's terribly boring."

"Perhaps you'll be able to swap him. Perhaps one of the GIs will ask you to dance."

71

"They don't dance like us. They fling themselves about, not a bit like we did in those classes. It's called jive, or jitterbugging, or some such name. Joy can do it. She says it's really
wizard. The man throws you about."

"Throws you?"

I wondered if that's how John danced. It sounded weird to me.

But when I went to do the National Savings the next Sunday Mrs Andrews said John was coming home. He arrived two days before the date of our dance.

TEN

To my amazement John agreed to come to the school dance without any persuading at all. I didn't even have to ask him, for Mrs Andrews had told him about it. What exactly she had told him I didn't like to think: something like 'that pathetic little girl across the road wants you to take her to a dance. She'll cry if you don't say yes.' But no, Mrs Andrews was very kind. She wouldn't sneer. Had John sighed in disbelief? But no, he gave no hint that it wasn't anything but a privilege to be asked to the school dance.

"Have to be on my best behaviour, eh?" I supposed he was thinking of jitterbugging.

"Lots of GIs are coming," I said.

"It should be quite lively then."

He smiled happily. I longed to ask him if he would wear his uniform, but I didn't dare. I knew he wouldn't. All the GIs would be in uniform. Their uniform was so smart: they all looked like officers, for a start; no wonder all the girls fell for them.

His car was playing up, he said, and we would have to go on the train --- another disappointment ---- but perhaps, I thought, we would get an empty carriage on the way home and he would hold my hand . . . perhaps. By the time the night came I was a nervous wreck. It was ten days before Christmas. We would break up for the holidays two days later and Peter would be home. My mother was going potty trying to work out how to make a Christmas pudding and cake and mince pies and things without any ingredients. John brought her a packet of sultanas and she was over the moon with joy. She had managed to lengthen my green dress with a false hem and although it wasn't a party dress it was the only thing I had that I liked. Shoes were a problem: I only had a pair of lace-ups and gym shoes. I had worn gym shoes for the dancing classes and my mother wouldn't let me spend any coupons on shoes for best: "There won't be enough. We all need new vests after Christmas and then it'll be sandals as soon as it gets warm. You hardly ever need best, it's not worth it." But Anne came up trumps with a pair of her auntie's that fitted and weren't too terrible, even though they were pre-war. Anne had best of her own and didn't want them. Her auntie's were black and shiny with silver buckles and slight heels. I wasn't used to heels but practised at home in the evenings and I really liked them. I had to give them back after the dance, unfortunately. I had to wear my school coat, of course, the only coat I had apart from my muddy farm jacket, but I didn't much care about that.

It was very cold on the night but luckily it wasn't raining. John called for me in time to catch the train. He wasn't in uniform but he was wearing his bomber jacket over his smart clothes because it was so cold. My mother saw us off with a doubting expression and told John not to miss the last train, but the dance was starting early and I guessed it would finish quite early too, knowing the mentality of our elders.

"It's only a school thing," I warned him. "No drink or anything."

"I don't think that will stop some of our friends," he said.

I saw what he meant later, as the GIs all brought hip-flasks.

Of course they didn't come till later. At the start the job lot of grammar school boys lined one of the walls all talking to each other and the girls all lined the opposite wall eying up the boys. The ones who had brought boys didn't dance because their boys were all too frightened to

start. John would have started: he asked me but I wouldn't. So quite a lot of the girls started dancing
together and then when the floor wasn't quite so empty the boys got bolder and started off. When John asked me again, I agreed. He was laughing.

"It was like this years ago, when I was at school," he said.

We launched off together. I was so frightened that I would tread all over him but he was so good he made it easy, better than anybody, even Colin, so that by two turns of the hall I was dancing with complete confidence in his arms feeling like Ginger Rogers, my head swirling with pride and joy. The old school hall, battered and boarded up as it was, looked rather marvellous with paper chains swinging across from its galleries (it had galleries all round the top of it) and its lights coloured in a rather nauseous fashion by party bulbs. The music that filled it, instead of hymns and the songs generally squeaked out by the choir ("With a Hey and a Ho and a Hey Nonny No") was strong and brassy, mostly Glenn Miller or smoochy Victor Sylvester, Jo Loss and his orchestra and, later, Scott Joplin. John and I were whizzing about to "Putting on Your Top Hat, Putting on the Style" and I was, for the first time in my life, finding out how lovely it was to dance with a good partner and have your feet doing the right thing without having to even think about it. John danced fast and held me tightly so that we never collided with anyone and I could see my friends looking impressed in the arms of the slowly clod-hopping grammar school boys. The staff recruited for the occasion, the younger ones (that is, not quite ready for retirement) stood round the walls looking worried or dispensed soft drinks in the library. Never had I felt so happy.

Annabel arrived with Monty. She looked fabulous, no doubt decked out by her sisters-in-law, in a dress of shimmering purple taffeta and high-heeled shoes, her hair newly set and wearing red lipstick. We all gaped. I saw her eyes rake round the competition, seeing none, until she saw John and me. That expression --- how well I knew it . . . ! John was lighting a cigarette and didn't see her. At the same moment Joy came in with her GI. Everything then went into another gear.

Joy's cowboy was about six foot six tall and radiated cheer and goodwill. Behind him came about ten of his friends, all out for a good time but obviously aware that this was a girls' school, not the Hammersmith Palais. They were extremely polite and careful, taking it all in --- no doubt amazed at the British way of doing things. Then one of them approached the boys on the platform doing the music and shortly afterwards Glenn Miller blasted out at twice the decibels we had had before and everyone was dancing at twice the speed and the whole atmosphere changed. I saw one of the GIs offering one of our staff a cigarette and she actually took it, and then he took out a hip flask and offered it to her as well, but this was a bit too much for her and I saw panic flare in her eyes. At the same time a GI came for me but John was already whisking me back on to the floor with a "Sorry, mate, this one's mine" and we were off again, no stopping. I had time to notice that no GI asked Annabel, even though Monty was doing nothing to claim her, just standing there gawping in dismay at the competition. She was looking furious. Good, good, good, I thought.

After that it all went rather wild. It was great. Even on lemonade I felt an amazing euphoria seizing me as we danced to the loud, fast music. The GIs had brought their own aura with them: a fierce intention to have a good time yet, even with the hip flasks to hand, they didn't get out of hand, no doubt aware that they were in with a crowd of innocent children. They were friendly and funny and polite but danced like demons. What a far cry from our lessons! Nobody had told us that in the right atmosphere it all came naturally, even the jitterbugging. After an hour or two we were flinging ourselves about, or being flung, with wild abandon, and I found out that yes, John knew all about jitterbugging. He was as good as any of the GIs

and far, far better than any of the grammar school boys, including Monty. He was quite at home with the GIs and smoked and chatted with them in the intervals, so that I too was included in this special hierarchy. There seemed a whole generation between these men and the grammar school boys, yet in truth it was only a few years. I noticed the staff dispensing the supper were having difficulty in accepting what was happening and were on tenterhooks for fear it might all fall apart, but one or two of the GIs were chatting them up in that easy American manner that seemed so natural to them and I could see that, with a few drinks inside them and a few decades knocked off their age they would be jitterbugging with the best. How strange all these revelations! In my narrow, self-absorbed, pony-soaked life I had never before experienced such feelings.

As it got later the music cooled and fell into the nostalgic wartime mode with "There'll be blue skies over the white cliffs of Dover" and "We'll meet again, don't know where, don't know when" which we all knew so well. They announced from the platform that we would have an Excuse-Me dance and as I fell into John's arms again without thinking, some one tapped me on the shoulder from behind with a curt "Excuse me" and I turned to see Annabel about to annexe my John. Of course for good manners he had to take her and I had to swap to fish-faced Monty, but luckily after a few turns of the hall Joy's GI claimed me and I was able to enjoy myself again. I asked him about being a cowboy and he told me how they worked, using a corral of horses: the work was so hard they had to have a lot, but you got to know your favourites, the ones who knew the job so well you didn't have to tell them what to do. I was very glad to be distracted. I couldn't see over his shoulder as he was too tall but I did get glimpses of John and Annabel, and saw that she was using all her charms as usual and that John was being really nice to her. Was that just good manners? How could I tell? But the next time I looked someone had excused her and John was with Anne, so I relaxed. Perhaps Anne was doing me a good turn, knowing my feelings about Annabel. But when the music had finished and we drifted back to our own partners John asked me the name of the girl he had been dancing with.

"Anne," I said.

"No, not that one. The first one, the one in purple."

"Gertrude Higginbottom," I said.

John laughed. He didn't believe me.

Then some one said we would have the last dance and put on "Goodnight Irene" which was nearly always the last dance and made you want to cry and John took me up again and held me close and we danced for the last time. I was so wound up and dizzy with emotion I just put my face in his chest and shut my eyes. He put his head down and I could feel his cheek on the top of my head. He didn't say anything. I felt like crying now yet I was so happy. I wanted it to go on for ever.

Of course it didn't. We had to catch the last train and the GIs had to get back to base and the staff had to clear up. We fetched our coats and walked back to he station. It was a fine night but very cold. Of course there were no lights showing save the moon and the stars which glittered above us. John was very quiet. I couldn't tell what he was thinking. The station was dark and empty and when our train came in we couldn't tell if there were any empty carriages as all the blinds were pulled down. Of course I had no idea if John wanted an empty carriage. (An empty carriage was just a schoolgirl thing. We used to run down the train looking and shouting, "Here's one! Here's one!" so that on our own we could shout and lark about and hang out of the window). We opened the nearest door and there were a couple of lovers in it so John shut the door and tried the next one and it had an elderly couple in so we joined them and sat in silence in the dim blue light. John wasn't used to the train and was thrown by there being no names on any of the stations, but I knew it so well I knew when it was our station.

"Lucky I've got my navigator with me," he said.

It was only ten minutes walk to home. I don't know what I expected. I had seen so many romantic films in my life when the couple bade farewell in the dark to the strains of beautiful music with a tender kiss, but John, after his jolly evening, now seemed wrapped in thoughts of his own. I had seen him like this before, only not often.

I asked him, "How much leave have you got? When are you going back?"

"Tomorrow."

Tomorrow! I had been thinking he was home for Christmas. I was bitterly disappointed.

"I was supposed to have Christmas off," he said. "But they've changed their minds. I'm sorry. We could have had fun . . . " His voice trailed away.

We were coming up our road to our houses. When we got to my gate he said, "It was lovely evening. I really enjoyed it. I'll come and say goodbye before I go, I promise."

And he put his arm round me and gave me a gentle hug. No kiss.

"Goodnight, my sweet."

And he crossed the road and let himself into his house with his key and was gone. I stood there alone in the dark. All the excitement of the evening had drained away and I was very cold. The stars and the crescent moon were sharp and bitter. I didn't want to go in. I knew my mother would be waiting up and Peter would be ready to bait me and laugh. It was absolutely silent, with just a faint smell of chimney smoke on the air and the bare garden trees outlined now with frost.

And then, as always, the sound of the bombers approaching, on their way to Germany, that familiar drone, far away, very high. Did John hear them? I think most people did not notice; it was a fact of life, but to me it was like my heart beating. I couldn't remember before the war any more. It seemed it would go on for ever, and I was going to stand there for ever, looking at the sky, waiting. To grow older.

* * *

John came to say goodbye as promised. He was full of spirits now, just as we knew him, laughing about whether his car would make the journey or he would end up absent without leave. He was in uniform this time, very smart, and when his aunt was kissing him goodbye she nodded at me and said to John, "Show her your pretty little badge."

"The caterpillar?"

He turned back his lapel and I saw pinned inside it a brooch of a little gold caterpillar with ruby eyes.

"The Caterpillar Club," his aunt said proudly. "You get one if you have to bale out."

"It's lovely!"

My parents admired it, and John shook hands with them.

"Look after yourself. Best of luck," they said, as if he were going on holiday.

He went back across the road to his car, pulled on the bomber jacket that was lying on the seat, kissed his aunt and uncle and then turned to me. He put his hands on my shoulders, smiled down at me and said, "Keep on growing older, it becomes you. We'll go dancing again next time."

And he put his arms round me and kissed me gently on the lips. Then he got in the car and drove away.

Mrs Andrews started to cry and her husband put his arm round her and took her indoors. I went on standing in the road like a zombie until my mother came out and shouted at me and then I went in for breakfast.

* * *

Before we broke up for Christmas we were told to put our names down for harvest camp in the summer if we wanted to go. The top forms had always done harvest camp and now we were old enough, strong enough, to take part. I think all schools did it as there were no men left to help with the harvest, mostly boys schools, I suppose, but our school had an arrangement with a farm on the Sussex downs. We heard that you worked with German prisoners. Our farmer, where Peter and I went, wouldn't have German prisoners. The camp was said to be very hard work but a great lark in the evenings; we had heard all the stories from the forms above. Lots of boys seemed to appear, they said. It lasted a fortnight and you slept in tents. The younger staff were recruited to run it and they weren't very strict. A lot of us put our names down, even Annabel, but not poor Biddy whose lungs could not cope with harvest. Because of Alan she wanted to be a farmer and already had her name down for an agricultural college when she left school. She was going to do cows and milking, which would not harm her. I was going to be a WAAF but everyone said the war would be over by the summer. Just my luck, I thought.

ELEVEN

Two days before Christmas I was helping my mother decorate a rather scrawny Christmas tree which my father had brought in. I think he had dug it up from somewhere: it was proving very hard to make it look pretty.

"It'll look all right when the candles are lit," my mother said hopefully.

Then she said, "Go upstairs and fetch those hair clips from my dressing-table. They'll be just the thing for fixing this paper."

I went upstairs. My mother's dressing table was in a bay window looking out over the road. I wasn't really looking but something unusual caught my eye: a boy on a bicycle cycling slowly on the wrong side of the road, peering at the house numbers. It was a telegraph boy in uniform. I snatched the net curtains aside and felt my heart turn over inside me. The telegraph boys brought the terrible news, delivering it to the door in a small brown envelope: "The War Office regrets to inform you . . " We all hated seeing telegraph boys. I stood there staring.

He was slowing right opposite our house. He stopped, got off and propped his bike against the Andrews' fence, opened the gate and went up the path. He knocked at the door. Mrs Andrews answered it, her hands floury with baking. I could not see her face exactly but I saw her take the envelope. The boy turned away and came back down the path. Mrs Andrews shut the door.

It was like watching a scene in a film. I was rooted to the spot in horror. It surely meant . . . or did people get telegrams for other reasons? Birthdays?

Was it Mrs Andrews' birthday? Was some one coming to stay? My father once got a telegram, something about work. But everyone knew the commonest reason for the telegraph boy calling.

I went downstairs and told my mother.

"A telegram boy has just called on Mrs Andrews."

My mother looked up, her face showing the same shock and horror as I was feeling. But then she got up and said briskly, "Don't fear the worst. If it's missing, they often turn up later."

She actually put an arm round me and said, "Let's not jump to conclusions, my pet. It could be anything."

But she had already betrayed that she thought it was about John.

After that we worked on the Christmas tree in silence, not really noticing much what we were doing. I felt the tears trickling down my cheeks and my mother was blowing her nose at intervals. It was getting dark and the sky was heavy with rain clouds. The house was freezing cold as we didn't light the fire until my father came home, trying to spin out the coal ration, so it was a totally cheerless evening. I found I was shivering. Crying and shivering.

My mother got up.

"Let's make a cup of tea. And I'll light the fire early."

She fetched my father's very old camel-hair dressing gown and wrapped it round me and gave me a peckish sort of kiss on my forehead. Did she know how I felt about John? He was just a family friend, she had always maintained, and much too old to take an interest in me. Did he take an interest in me? Perhaps now I would never know.

My father came home and we told him what had happened. He looked very sad.

"Poor lad, if it's true. To have lasted so long and now that it's nearly over . . ."

"Perhaps we should enquire," my mother suggested. "Will you go over and find out? It's not being nosey. We need to know."

My father agreed. He went out but we couldn't see anything because of the dark. The faintest blue light showed the opening of the front door, and as it then closed and he didn't come back we assumed he had been asked in. I don't think he had ever been in their house before. Mostly people didn't ask their neighbours in. The Andrews are the only people who asked me in when I did the National Savings; all the rest left me on the doorstep. I remembered my first sight of John in the lovely photograph in their living-room and how I had fallen in love then when I was eleven. Four years ago --- how faithful I had been!

My father came back half an hour later. We could see immediately that our fears were confirmed.

"Yes. The telegram reports his plane as missing. It didn't return. But that still leaves a good margin for hope so it's not total doom and gloom. Mr Andrews gave me a whisky and said he was bound to turn up. He might well have baled out again --- who knows?"

The whisky had obviously given my father the same optimism as Mr Andrews had revealed.

"He might be a prisoner of war if he baled out over Germany. Sometimes it takes ages for the news to come through," my mother said.

"He could easily have baled out and be with our own forces. In which case the news should come through quite soon."

Was it only myself who feared the worst? I could not help recalling John's strange mood after the dance, as if he himself was mulling over his own mortality: to have been lucky for so long . . . by the law of averages, luck did not last for ever. It was not in the nature of an intelligent man not to give it thought.

I had to do the National Savings the next day, on Christmas eve, a Sunday. I fetched my stamps and Miss Eburne said to me, "Give the Andrews my best wishes for good news. Give them my love." The whole road was sad, you could feel it.

It wasn't my imagination. It was Christmas but no one was laughing. I was totally distraught about calling on the Andrews, and when Mrs Andrews opened the door I fell inside and burst out sobbing, I couldn't help it. Mrs Andrews took me in her arms and hugged me.

"There, there, my love. Don't take it so hard! It's not all lost yet. You have to have faith."

Mr Andrews pulled a chair up to the fire and gave me a golden drink in a little glass. Over his shoulder I could see the gorgeous photo of John smiling at me, as if to cheer me up. As if to say. "I'll soon be home."

For all their comforting words and kindness I could see that the news had changed the old couple: they both looked haggard in a way I had never seen before. They kept saying that missing could mean anything, and I knew this was true. I had heard all the stories of pilots walking in weeks later, and I knew it took a long time for news to come through about men who had been taken prisoner.

Mr Andrews said, "No one actually saw the plane go down, apparently. It just didn't come back to base. So it could have crash-landed somewhere, or they could have baled out miles from anywhere. We don't know, do we? We could get news any minute."

If only, I thought! More likely news of a crashed plane full of bodies. There were ten crew in a Flying Fortress. I knew all the jobs they did and where they sat, how the most dangerous job was that of tail gunner as the tail quite often got shot off and the man died alone. I knew all this because of Peter. He knew everything about planes.

I pulled myself together and sold Mrs Andrews her stamps and when I departed she kissed me.

"Keep your pecker up, lovey."

* * *

It was bitterly cold. Peter came home and our news squashed even his high spirits and the whole road was quiet and sad. It was a strange Christmas. Toasts were made to it being the last wartime Christmas; people could not believe how long it had lasted, when all the forecasts at the start had been 'it'll be over by Christmas' --- they had meant the first one, back in nineteen thirty-nine. I did the National Savings as usual on the Sunday but the Andrews had no more news. That made it about ten days since the telegram. I could see that they were losing hope fast. They both looked ten years older with all the stuffing knocked out of them. We didn't cry again but I felt so close to them, it was very strange. I felt ten years older too: I had grown up just as John had wanted. Because he had died.

Mrs Andrews said, "After all, now we know how it feels, you have to remember we are just one of millions since this terrible war started. Millions have felt like we do now. It doesn't bear thinking about. And still that man refuses to surrender even when he knows he's finished. So how many more will have to die before he himself dies? How many more thousands?"

I had never had occasion to pull my head out of the sand and think hard about this truth; I only thought about the war in how it affected me, so cushioned was I by the fact that I had no close relations or dear family friends in the forces save John. But at school we were all the same: in prayers every morning we were directed to think of our brave forces and so we did for a moment or two but mostly I know I was more impatient to see if my name was down for the hockey team than in wondering how far our men had advanced across France. We had grown up with the war and took it for granted. The war was the background to our lives: we lived every day for the trivial larks we played on each other, the bitching over friendships, the delight in getting good marks, the queasy fear of having to admit that you hadn't done your French homework. . . nothing to do with war at all. The war was just having horrible food and not enough coupons for clothes and always being freezing cold, things you took for granted but which in no way stopped you having fun. But for the first time now it had all changed.

School was just the same and if I now felt I had turned into a different person no one noticed it. As the days went past and all hope for John died I went on going to school and when I was in school nothing was any different: the lessons, the bickering, the games matches and laughing and fighting and getting into trouble, all as usual, until getting home and seeing the quiet house across the road and going to bed at night and thinking about the bombers.

But soon the lullaby of the bomber engines fell silent, for in the spring the war in Europe was declared over and we all went mad with joy and we had a great bonfire and party in the middle of the road (which melted it and made a great hole in the middle) and a bomber flew over shooting off red Verey lights and the searchlights danced all over the sky at midnight and Churchill spoke on the radio and the King spoke and the bands played in the parks and I went to bed at midnight every night exhausted with singing and dancing.

And three days after these celebrations Mr Andrews came over and spoke to my father and when he had gone my father told us that the remains of John's Flying Fortress had been discovered burnt out, deep in a wood in Germany with all the crew dead inside it. They were to be buried in the nearest graveyard with full military honours, amongst other fallen British dead, all soldiers.

So that was the end, the end of the war and the end of John.

TWELVE

The fact that the war was over made no difference, after the first celebrations, to our school timetable which remained the same: first our terrible exams, the School Certificate, and then, on breaking up, the farm camp in Sussex. There were no men home yet to go back to farming (should they wish to after their five year absence) and the harvest still depended on school children, elderly labourers and the German prisoners who, it seemed, were not to be sent home in a hurry. The war with Japan was still continuing, of course, and we all knew that the Japanese, like Hitler, did not believe in surrender, even when it was quite obvious that they were beaten. The Americans were taking the brunt of the fighting over there but Joy's cowboy was safe in Germany and, apparently, having a great time. Joy missed him terribly.

Did I miss John? I cannot truly say that my real grief lasted for very long. I could see that for the Andrews it was going to last for ever, but for myself John had played quite a small part in my life. Those cheerful leaves were scattered amongst my real life like stars whose light was fading as dawn crept over the sky. My everyday life of school and friendships was entirely consuming: the highlights were now made up of expeditions that had been denied us so long, to the seaside to play and go swimming off the beach now cleared of barbed wire fences, to London to see plays with great actors, (gorgeous Laurence Olivier!) to the art galleries to see all the pictures that had returned after languishing in Welsh quarries all through the war. And, after the exams were over, the excitement of our first harvest camp in Sussex, which we were informed by the classes above us who had already been was fantastic for boys. "They come up in the evening, from all around. It's amazing. And some of the prisoners are smashing. They aren't allowed to talk to us, but . . . " (giggle, giggle). We couldn't wait.

We were all going, all my friends, except Biddy (too wheezy to cope with harvest) ---- but including Annabel, unfortunately. But even if she hived off the most desirable, it sounded as if there would be enough boys to go round.

Perhaps even if John had been there to come home on leave I would have been hard put to to take time off to go out with him, for the work and revision for our exams was unrelenting. When they actually arrived it was quite a relief. Biddy was so wheezy at this time that she came and went every day in a taxi, poor Biddy. I actually enjoyed doing the exams, unburdening myself of the great heap of knowledge that had been drummed into me for so long, wondering whether I would ever need to speak Latin in later life or know what was the chief export of Madagascar when I was married and had four children. But of course the brain is trained and expanded by this pounding it gets in youth and the work ethic is planted --- or so my father explained it when I used to cry over my homework. But after the exams were over it was bliss.

Harvest camp wasn't compulsory but all my friends put down for it. It would last a fortnight and we were to sleep in tents in a wonderful place up on the downs. There were about twenty of us, in charge of two teachers: one a young innocent thing who had only just arrived at our school and the other a nice old biddy who liked country life and was never known to have told anybody off in her life. They didn't have to cook. The farmer had arranged some women to cook for us and we ate in his barn, but our tents were far enough away from the farm not to be overlooked. We had to go to the farm for work at eight in the morning and we finished at five, with an hour off for lunch. We were told that the farmer was very strict. This information came from the class above us. They were going off somewhere else.

Just before we were due to go the rumour went round that the Japanese had offered to surrender. It was all a bit vague. Was the war over or not? Apparently the Americans had dropped a terrible new bomb on them, the bomb to end all bombs. And if they did not surrender they would drop another one. If the Japanese had agreed to surrender when asked earlier the bomb would not have been dropped. The Americans had got tired of the slaughter of their troops out there, all for no reason when it was quite obvious that the Japanese were beaten. I couldn't help thinking that if this amazing bomb had been available earlier and been dropped on Hitler we too would have had our European war over much more quickly and my dear John would still be alive now, along with thousands of other men.

But this was not uppermost in our minds when we collected on Victoria station with our luggage and bicycles to make the journey to Sussex. Annabel had her working gear packed: the most elegant overalls known to man, set off with a belt from Harrods and a silk scarf elegantly, negligently, tossed round her shoulders. The rest of us seemed to have our brothers' cast-off trousers and our own faded Aertex shirts with sweat-stained armpits --- "You only want your old stuff for that sort of work," our mothers said.

What about all these boys we were going to meet? We surreptitiously packed a nice skirt (mine was made out of some old summer curtains) and a clean blouse and --- how daring! --- our Tangee lipsticks. We filled three carriages and laughed and screamed all the way to Sussex, where we were decanted at a very small station somewhere beyond Lewes. An old bus was there to meet us but there was nowhere to put the bicycles, so we bicyclists set off with a map drawn rather arbitrarily by the bus driver. At least we had an address if our map reading let us down although we had been well-taught to read maps at school. But the bus driver's map was far removed from the Ordnance Survey. We argued at cross-roads; some decided to go one way

and others another, and soon Anne and I found ourselves bowling along alone, brimming with pure joy. The sun was shining: a world of sun-dappled downs dipped and swung all round us, so fresh and open after the Surrey woods and commons that our bicycles knew so well. Distant glimpses of the sea flickered between hedgerows and the sky was loud with the song of skylarks: it was heaven ---- freedom! Exams all forgotten! The war over! A fortnight of honest endeavour beckoning ahead and boys to meet --- boys! What larks!

We found our farm by seeing a clutch of army tents set up in a field on the side of a valley which we decided must be for us. There were four to a tent so Anne and I bagged one and for our pains got Annabel sharing, and Joy. No one else wanted Annabel and it was Anne's magnanimity that invited her, not mine. Anne was always a saint and such a comfort for a friend when you had argued and fallen out with all the others. Living together for a fortnight was bound to result in all sorts of squabbles and bitching so it was lovely to have Anne's imperturbability to hand. I feared the worst with Annabel when the boys arrived.

Our two staff, Jonesy and Piggy, had a tent to themselves. They had a tough time refereeing all the complications of who shared a tent with whom, but when it was all over we saw them in their tent sitting in deck-chairs, smoking. Amazement! Our camp was on a hillside that sloped down into a valley. The farmhouse and farm buildings were in the valley. Both sides of the valley had been ploughed for the exigencies of wartime (ancient chalk downland!) and were now bearing the crops that we were here to harvest. Already there was a tractor at work with a reaper behind it, driven by --- yes! ---- a boy! Somebody had had the brilliant idea of bringing a pair of binoculars, so we all took it in turns to look. He wasn't bad.

"Common," said Annabel.

"Nice hair," said Joy.

Slightly up from the farm there was an old deserted house that must once have been the
original farmhouse. We all went to explore and found that it boasted a real lavatory with a chain that pulled . Eureka! We had already given the thumbs down to the rickety Elsans that lurked behind a hessian screen at the top end of our campsite, so this was quite a find. We were told later that the house was haunted, so when we went to use the proper lavatory it came to be known as going haunting. "I'm just going haunting." There was no water laid on in the camp so washing was not going to be a problem, no washing. But Jonesy and Piggy made us fetch water in buckets each morning from the farm and doled out washing-up bowls, one to each tent, so there was the possibility of a quick dab with a flannel. We had to be ready for work at eight, breakfast at seven.

Of course none of us slept that first night, not finding our army truckle beds and straw palliases the acme of comfort. At least we had our air-raid shelter sleeping bags and siren suits like Winston Churchill so were not cold. Only Annabel who had a lacy night-dress.

"Who does she think is going to see her?" was the question.

It was very cold as dawn started to slide silvery fingers across the top of the downs. I lay with my head by the open flap sniffing the wonderful smell of the wet grass and listening to the first skylarks that were starting to whirr up singing into the sky. No longer the drone of the bombers, but the music of skylarks, and I thought of John missing all this. That day on Epsom downs, as he lay silent, had he been wondering if he would live to enjoy such days again? How could it be otherwise? He must have known . . . his luck had lasted so long. And although I was full of excitement and longing to start this new day I could not help shedding a few tears again for John who had had such an appetite for life. And all the others who would not see a dawn come up and hear the skylarks again. I was glad that the terrible bomb had put a stop to it. If only it had come earlier!

Breakfast was a bit of a blow --- porridge, thick and slimy without sugar, only milk. Nobody had any sugar, of course, not even a farm. But at least it had lots of butter and the bread was nice. While we were eating, the farmer, Mr Paul, came in to address us. He wasn't a bit like the farmer where Peter and I went, but quite a business-like man, getting on a bit, dressed in good clothes, not conspicuously friendly.

"You're here to do a job, remember, not just play about. You can play about after work, not in my time. Today you will be stooking. When you've finished your meal the boys will give you a lesson in how to make a good stook. It's no good to me if you don't do it properly --- a wind comes up in the night and in the morning it's all on the ground --- I won't be best pleased."

Nothing about how nice to have us and he hoped we'd be happy, etc. When he said the boys will give you a lesson we all perked up and nudged each other and giggled but a heavy glance from his sour eyes soon put a stop to it. Talk about being back at school!

So after breakfast we all trooped out to the field where the reaping was going on and had our first introduction to barley. It lay on the ground in sheaves tied with cord. Stooking meant picking up four sheaves and stacking them stalks down, heads together, in such a way that they stood upright and got dried by the sun and the wind. It looked easy but it wasn't easy to stand them properly so that they didn't fall down

The boy on the tractor, who was called Les, came forward to demonstrate, along with his mate Cyril. They were waiting to be called up and had never been off the farm in their lives.

Blushing furiously, they picked up a couple of sheaves each, stood them up and rammed their heads together, then another pair to make a foursome. This was then a stook.

"Try it," they said.

We all waded in. The jokers put them upside down and the cunning ones said, "Show me" and fluttered their eyelashes. Annabel wasn't interested as Les and Cyril were too common for her. After the farmer had gone in to his breakfast we found that Les and Cyril were great fun and we had a hilarious time playing at stooking. Even with our best efforts they all slithered to the ground.

Les said, "You'd better buck your ideas up when the guv'nor comes out."

It was clear they were frightened of the guv'nor.

"Like this, you ignorant loonies," they said. "If you don't get it right we'll get skinned."

So we tried. After eight hours, at the end of the day, we were beginning to get the hang of it. We were also half-dead, starving, covered in barley barbs and finding it hard to believe that this 'holiday' had been sold to us as terrific fun. Luckily most of us were very fit and after a quite eatable tea of corned beef hash and jelly we found ourselves slowly recovering. A long evening of doing nothing on the sun-drenched hillside seemed a good idea. But when we got back to camp Jonesy and Piggy said we'd all been invited to a big house up the road which belonged to 'an old girl'. This meant an old girl of our school. We were a bit doubtful and some elected not to go, but about ten of us decided to risk it. The others chose to wait for the boys Les and Cyril had promised would soon put in an appearance.

We cleaned up a bit with a bucket of water and brushed the barley out of our hair and set off on our bicycles, or on foot, for the big house. It was about two miles away, farther than we thought, and us with bicycles gave the others a lift, two to a bike, which resulted in several of us colliding or falling in the ditch. This made for some hilarity and dishevelment so that we had to stop and pull ourselves together when we came to the driveway of a very large and elegant house. It stood some way off the road and was surrounded with fenced paddocks. We stood looking at it doubtfully, not sure if we had made the right choice in coming.

"The old girl done good," Joy said.

In one of the paddocks two ponies grazed. One was a beautiful grey Arab and the other a chestnut. My heart soared .

"Oh look! How fantastic!"

Of course the others weren't interested in horses, not even Annabel who only gave the creatures a fleeting glance. I dallied along the drive to make friends as the two ponies came to the fence to goggle at us, and stood talking to them for a bit. They just looked so beautiful standing there, the last of the evening sun gilding their fine summer coats and the downs rolling away behind them with the sea in the distance, I was transfixed with happiness. I was in no hurry to go on my way, shy now at the thought of entering this imposing mansion even if my friends had gone before me. They had disappeared round the corner of the house.

"Are you looking for some one?" a voice behind me

said.

I jumped round in surprise and found myself being examined by a boy. He looked about eighteen or nineteen and was on a bike, like me, presumably coming home. He looked as if he had been doing the same work as us, with barley barbs sticking out of his jersey and his brown face furred with dust. He had dirty-looking fair hair, tousled and rather long, and rather sharp grey eyes, and he was very handsome. He would be pounced upon if he continued his journey up to the house.

"We've been invited," I said. "I got left behind, talking to your ponies. The others have gone ahead."

"You're from Mr Paul's camp?"

"Yes. Your ponies are lovely."

"Yeah, they're my sister's, but she's away at the moment."

We walked on together, pushing our bikes.

"I've been working at Clives --- that's the farm beyond Paul's. He's not such a hard task-master as old Paul, and he pays better too. Barley's a pig, isn't it? Is that what you're doing?"

"Yes. It's nearly killed us."

"You'll get some mothering here. Last year, my ma had them all in, she loves it, talking about her old school. She's a bit batty, you'll see."

It seemed I had collared the only boy for miles around without even trying, for when we walked round the side of the house together we found all my friends disposed about a beautiful terrace drinking lemonade out of tall glasses and eating home-made biscuits with chocolate icing. The batty mother beamed a welcome, saying to her son, "Oh you filthy boy! And all these nice girls come to visit! This is my son Con, he's farming too at the moment --- you'll have to excuse him."

She was very elegant, like her house, and had obviously been nowhere near a barley field but spent her time cooking these delicious biscuits. (What with, for heaven's sake?). I sank into the garden chair she pulled out for me and Con helped himself to a handful of biscuits and made no move to go and get washed.

"We're all rather dirty too," we said, not caring, and I saw Con being appraised by a circle of predatory eyes. How strange, I thought, that all of us were wearing our old grey shorts and faded Aertexes except for Annabel, who was wearing a plain but very becoming flowered dress. Her eyes were resting on Con in a way I knew so well. I could tell that she was interested. Although dirty, Con was far from common, a public schoolboy, no doubt, in the same league as Monty but with more brain and a chin. I saw him first, I wanted to say. I didn't stand a chance.

Elizabeth (she said, "Call me Elizabeth,") said to me, 'Did you get left behind, dear?"

"I stopped to speak to your ponies. They are so beautiful."

"Ah yes, they belong to my daughter Deirdre, but she's away all the summer. Poor Con is having to keep them exercised, he promised her. Do you ride then, dear? You could help him, you could ride together."

As I opened my mouth to reply Annabel cut in. "I ride," she said.

"Oh, that's splendid! Con would be so pleased to have some help."

"I ride too," I squeaked, but no one heard me.

Con was eyeing up Annabel, I could see, and she was sitting there smirking. I knew she had her jodhpurs in her luggage, (her elegant Swaine, Adeney and Briggs pair bought in Piccadilly) and she was just seeing herself cavorting on that heavenly Arab with Con's adoring eyes upon her. The others were all thinking this too and goggling with bemusement: did she know how much we all hated her? She didn't care, of course.

"Whenever it suits you, I'll come up," she said.

I guessed she would too, even in Mr Paul's working time.

"Six o'clock?" Con said.

"In the evening?"

"No. In the morning."

She didn't bat an eyelid. She must have felt our collected glee at her getting caught out like this, but she shrugged and said, "Fine."

Con grinned and disappeared indoors. I said to her, "It'll kill you, getting up at five after all that work today."

"Worth it," she said. "For him."

I would have got up at four.

He didn't reappear, no doubt shy at holding his own with such a bunch of predatory girls and his mother Elizabeth kept plying us with titbits (where did she get the stuff from?) and lemonade and asking us questions about 'the dear school' and eventually we had to go before we all fell asleep in her garden chairs.

"Come again!" she trilled. "We'll have a party at the weekend."

We rolled home.

"Are you really going up there in the morning?" I asked Annabel as we got into our sleeping bags.

"Of course," she said coolly. I noticed she was setting a little travelling alarm clock and had laid out her jodhpurs ready, along with a figure-hugging white jersey.

I hated her so much.

As it happened we never heard her alarm clock and were deeply asleep when Jonesy and Piggy roused us: they were late too and in a bit of a panic, so no one had time to wash. They didn't notice Annabel was missing. Our breakfast was waiting for us as we tore down the hill, moaning at the stiffness in our backs from all the bending of the day before. There was no sign of Annabel. We were already stooking when she rolled up, dressed in her working clothes. Mr Paul waylaid her as she came into the field, presumably to remonstrate, but we could see her looking at him with the amused contempt she used for all dressing-downs from higher authority. Poor Mr Paul.

Much as I would have liked to ignore her I couldn't help myself asking her, even while I despised myself, what it had been like.

"Nice ride," she said airily. And then, "Nice boy too."

She gave a smug smile and hefted her first two sheaves.

"I'm going again tomorrow."

I spent the morning consumed with jealousy. Not just the gorgeous boy, but the two gorgeous horses as well. Because I was working near Annabel (I presumed) Les came over on the tractor to chat us up. The tractor was flying a Union Jack on its bonnet.

"What's that for?" I asked.

"The war's over," Les said.

"Nobody told us!"

"It's not exactly official. Just pending," he said. "I'm all prepared. Even our lord and master has gone off to town to buy fireworks. The old skinflint is going to have a party."

"Blimey!"

"You're all invited." He eyed Annabel who was continuing, po-faced, with her stooking.

"You want to come out with me tonight on my motor-bike?"

"No fear," said Annabel.

"I'll come," I said.

I tried to work out if his face dropped, but his big blunt peasant's face (Annabel called him a peasant) turned to me happily and said, "Yeah, super. Across the fields --- I haven't got a license. See you then."

The tractor went snorting and smoking back into reaping and Anne said, "Crikey, what have you got yourself into?"

"I like motor bikes."

I liked Les and Cyril too. They were a laugh, like Peter's

101

friends. I had to have some consolation after losing the gorgeous Con. The others who hadn't gone to Elizabeth's house last night all said yes, boys did appear mysteriously out of the bushes when dusk fell, pinging the tents with blackberries, but Piggy and Jonesy chased them away. The message was, apparently, "See you in town."

What town? Some one said it was only a few miles down the valley: a small seaside town, not Brighton, just a little one, but it had pubs and a beach and the boys. I think it was called Seaford. Yippee everyone said. Annabel said she was going back to Elizabeth's. She had been asked for supper. We all made retching noises. I wanted to cry.

But by suppertime we were all nearly dead again and only wanted to lie out in the evening sun groaning. Annabel had departed, with permission from Jonesy and Piggy and I had forgotten my date with Les until he came revving into the field on a terrible old banger. Luckily Jonesy and Piggy had gone down to Mr Paul's for drinks so I got on the back and we whizzed off.

The fields were now all stubble, dipping and rolling away on either side of the river valley and Les opened the bike up and we went flying away down the shaved hill with a noise like a doodlebug, leaping over the bumps and drains with me screaming blue murder and Les laughing his head off. It was terrific. Peter would have loved it.

I think Les's bike was souped up for the crackle of its exhaust must have been heard in Brighton and its speed over the rough stubble was amazing. Of course we landed up at the bottom of the valley on the edge of the town where I found half our gang already being entertained by 'the boys'. Les left his bike in a hedge and we joined the crowd on the seafront.

Everyone was out wondering whether the war was over or not. Nobody seemed to know but assumed officialdom was still trying to put it into the right words. All this mattered apparently.

Les introduced us to Duffer and Jimmy and Glen and Alan and a load of others whose faces got completely mixed up: I was so tired I wanted to die. In the dusk the sea was rolling in soft waves up the stony beach, bringing the smell of freedom: I was feeling a little light-headed. I knew I had the ride back up the valley to survive before I could seek the blessing of my straw paliasse.

But Les rode sedately this time. Above the noise of the engine he asked me what was the name of my friend, the one who acts like the Queen.

"Gertrude Higginbottom," I said. Then, spitefully, thinking of that gorgeous Arab and the even more gorgeous Con, I said, "She thinks you're common."

Yeah," said Les happily, "I am."

And he laughed and opened up the throttle and we went hurtling home.

THIRTEEN

It wasn't done with trumpets or a fly-past of Spitfires or a gun salute. It was Mr Paul banging on the table with his porridge spoon and saying, "Girls, the war is over. You may have the day off."

After a moment's astonished silence, we all leapt up shouting and screaming. We hugged each other and danced about and the milk jug got knocked over and the porridge got cold and we didn't care. It was official! The war was over!

It was just starting to rain, to celebrate the day, so after we had cleared the tables and taken the dishes to the farmhouse we went and sat in the barn with Les and Cyril and they told us all about watching the Battle of Britain over their heads in the days of their youth and then they suggested we went and talked to the Jerries working on the neighbouring farm. Perhaps they didn't know yet? Annabel hadn't come back from riding, no doubt now celebrating with Con in style --- I didn't dare let my thoughts dwell on it ---- so I trailed up the field with my own gang and Les and Cyril and met the German prisoners who obviously hadn't been given the day off like us. They were weeding cabbages and were very pleased to see us. We shook hands all round and I didn't know what to say, even in English, let alone in German because, after all, we had won, hadn't we? But they seemed just as happy about it as us, and we could tell they were talking about us in German but we only knew Latin and French so didn't know what they were saying. They laughed a lot and a jolly fat one called Hermann showed us photos of his wife and children -- "Soon to see!" --- and a slim sad one with red hair called Rupert said he had no home to go back to as all his family had been killed in Dresden. This rather stymied our high spirits so Les suggested we leave them to their cabbages and we all go to town. It was raining harder now and by the time we got there we were all soaked through, but there was a big bonfire burning in the middle of the high street and lots of fireworks going off so we danced about with all the boys and sang "There'll Always be an England" while the rain ran down the backs of our necks and our socks steamed when we went to warm up by the fire. Duffer came and held my hand and said he loved me and would I come to the pictures with him on Saturday: he would fetch me in his car. A car! I was bowled over but Anne said Jonesy and Piggy wouldn't let me and I remarked (accurately) that they hadn't yet stopped us doing anything at all, where were they in fact?

Unfortunately they chose this moment to arrive amongst the festivities to round us up, as orders had come from above (our headmistress!) to say we all had to go to church that evening to give thanks. This meant incredible difficulty in making ourselves look like churchgoers. We hadn't washed for two days and our only best clothes were screwed up in rucksacks under the outer tent flap, all very damp and horrible. Of course when we reported for duty to catch an old bus that had been commandeered for us, looking like skinned rabbits and smelling of mould, Annabel appeared out of the blue completely dry and totally elegant in her black market costume complete with white gloves and a handbag.

"Where've you been all day?"I hissed.

"I was out to lunch in Brighton," she said. Then she added, "When I ride with Con, he keeps calling me Gertrude."

There was a questioning rise to her voice at this statement but I only said, "How strange," very nonchalantly, and Anne and the others got the giggles with lots of snorting. We didn't know where we were going: some sort of cathedral somewhere, I supposed, but we only went a little way to a small church all by itself in the country and by the time we had all filed in it was absolutely full. Jonesy and Piggy made us stay at the back and I was nearly out of the door. I could see the Pauls and Con's family at the front and even Les and Cyril and the cooking ladies and I felt very homesick and wished I was back with my mother and father and Peter, probably not in church but all being glad together. It had been such a long time and now it was over. I belonged at home. This made me feel weepy and I got my handkerchief out (it was wet and horrible) and then something amazing happened. Just as the vicar got up to start the service some one pressed my shoulder and said, "Budge up a bit,"and it was Con smiling down at me. I slithered along the seat and made him a few inches and he squeezed in so that his lovely warm (dry) thigh was pressed hard against mine. I forgot all about being homesick and nearly swooned with delight. Anne gave me a great dig with her elbow and started snorting again and I could see the nudges and whispers flickering across the rows the school occupied.

But it was a very solemn occasion and I found that after a little while I forgot about Con's warm thigh and my mind started to rove over the walls of the ancient church and take in the brass plaques silently remembering local men who died in the Great war, and in strange places I did not know about like Mysore and Vereeniging. I could see up by the altar the most beautiful sarcophagus of a mediaeval knight who had died at Agincourt. He lay there with a little dog at his feet and his wife by his side, reminding us that it went back for ever, dying in foreign parts for one's country. He too had ridden over these downs and worked his land like Mr Paul, might have even lived on the same site as Mr Paul's house, for we had been told it had mediaeval foundations. He seemed very close, like one of the congregation. An eerie late burst of sunshine after all the rain was now shining through the stained glass windows, and as the congregation rose to its feet to sing it seemed to me that we too were all made of coloured glass: we weren't people at all, just a great amorphous bowl hefting out those magnificent words: "Sun and moon bow down before him" which at the best of times made me feel faint with wonder. And feeling faint was the nub of the matter for I then passed out, crumpling down on to my Women's Institute hassock like one of our unsatisfactory stooks in a strong wind.

Afterwards they all said I did it on purpose because Con picked me up and carried me out of the church. But I never even knew this for when I came to a few minutes later I was lying on a wooden bench in the church porch with Jonesy hovering over me and Con's mother Elizabeth remonstrating with her : "Why, her clothes are all damp and her coat is soaked through. It's enough to give her pneumonia!"

Jonesy said, "It's just her age. They go down like ninepins at the drop of hat."

(Had she been drinking? Celebrations had been going on all day.)

"That well may be, but she needs some warmth and a strong cup of tea. Con, you run her home in my car and light the fire in the study and make sure she gets something inside her. She can't go back to a wet tent in this condition. I've got to get back, I've got to read the lesson."

"Okay ma," said Con.

At this I started taking notice, the fog leaving my brain.

"Oh please --- " I was going to say I didn't want to be a nuisance, but then I thought yes I did, if it meant going back alone with Con to his house. So I bit my tongue and stood up bravely and followed Con to Elizabeth's old heap in the car park. Con opened the door for me.

"I'm all right really," I said after he had got the car on the road and was heading home. "I don't know why I did that."

I did actually, as I remembered a very strange drink that Duffer had given me some time during the afternoon and Les later had produced some cider that he had made himself, so I suppose those drinks had confused my brain. Easily done, I wasn't used to drink. Nobody at home ever drank, only tea.

"It's okay," Con said. "I only went to church because ma ordered me to."

I sat there imagining what my friends must be thinking about my amazing luck while they were listening to a no doubt very long sermon, sitting there in their equally damp and unhealthy clothes and longing for a warm fire. How kindly fate had treated me!I had been getting into very tangled thoughts before I passed out and they came back to me as I sat waiting for my hot cup of tea, watching the flames starting to eat the kindling in the fireplace.

"I am sorry you had to leave the service," I said when he came back with the tea.

"I didn't mind. Not at all. I don't go to church unless forced."

"But today . . . it was different. To remember those who died. Not like communion or something."

Communion always gave me the creeps, drinking blood and all that. It had been explained to me at school in great detail but I still found it hard to take on board. I had always found, right from being little, Jesus on the cross a very disturbing image and I tried to blank it out, which wasn't easy considering how all the time it was pushed under one's nose. But sitting in church thinking about things and singing "Sun and moon bow down before him" and thinking of heaven up in the clouds --- I loved all that part of it. I obviously had a very simple mind. And now my mind in its simplicity would not leave what it was thinking before I passed out and instead of rejoicing in having Con all to myself I could only think of John being killed and Rupert having no family to go home to and I started to cry. It was so truly terrible, what had happened. I had danced through my childhood, untouched, and now felt deeply ashamed, sorry, sorry . . .

I said sorry through my sniffles but Con said, "It's all right. Don't worry."

I suppose I got something out of my system ("Hysteria, it's her age," Jonesy would have said) and after a bit I calmed down and wiped my face with my wet handkerchief and picked up my teacup. I knew I must have been a real turn-off and had blown any chance I had ever had with Con, but there was nothing to be done about it. At least he hadn't taken advantage and tried to comfort me with cuddles.

"Did you lose somebody?" he asked.

"Yes, just a little while ago when it was nearly over. I did love him."

He sat staring into the fire with his cup of tea.

"I wanted so much to be in it, always angry that I was born too late. Funny, isn't it? My brother was killed early on, in Africa, but it made no difference to how badly I wanted to be part of it."

This gave me a terrible jolt and made me feel worse than ever. A brother! And Elizabeth, to whom the service must have meant a great deal, so practically disposing of me before she went back to read the lesson, with all those emotions no doubt coursing through her stalwart brain . . . how relieved she must be that Con was to be deprived of his ambition. If my thoughts, prompted by the service, were in a tangle, however must she be feeling, mourning one son and rejoicing for another?

"Oh, gosh, I'm so sorry."

I would have done anything, then, not to have imposed on this kind family with my stupid hysteria. But the strong tea and the comforting flames were achieving their purpose and perhaps Con was happy enough to be delivered from the church. He was spruced up with a tie on and his hair tidy and he looked every bit as desirable as I remembered

109

him. After a bit he grinned at me and said, "Better?" and I nodded and said again that I was sorry to which he replied, "God's will. Circumstances beyond control. I'm glad it was you and not Gertrude Higginbottom."

I choked into my teacup at this and put it down with a rattle.

"She doesn't faint," I muttered.

"Poor Gertrude," he said.

Poor was an adjective it would never have occurred to me could be applied to Annabel, but it suggested a less than inflamed ardour on Con's part which rather cheered me up. Pity was the last emotion Annabel wished to provoke, I was sure. I didn't want to talk about her.

"Ma's having a party at the weekend," Con said. "She's going to invite you lot as well as all the family, but there's going to be a big party in town as well and old skinflint Paul says he's having one so you'll be spoilt for choice. I think you should come to ours," he added.

"Oh good, yes, super."

"Uncle Albert's coming. He's great at parties."

It didn't sound as if Mr Paul was going to get his moneysworth out of our camp with all these parties pending. I still felt very mixed up and homesick and shivery and Con said, "I'm sure ma will make you stay the night here when she comes back."

This idea seemed quite wonderful to me, as I did still feel rather peculiar and no one could say that there was anything inviting about spending the night in the tent on a cold hillside in the pouring rain when I could have a bed in this plushy warm house. Con was right as when his mother came in she told me she had already told Jonesy that I wouldn't be back till morning, and she took me briskly up to Deirdre's room and put a hotwater bottle in the bed and laid out a beautiful night dress.

"You'll be as right as rain in the morning."

"I'm sorry I interrupted the service for you."

110

"No, dear. It was of no consequence. These things happen."

I wanted to tell her that it was my thoughts that did it, rather than my age as diagnosed by Jonesy, but it was too difficult to put into words and I was now nearly asleep standing up. She bustled away and I got into bed.

Although I was so sleepy, I stayed awake long enough to savour my surroundings, as Deirdre's bedroom in the summer dusk was a treasure house, rosettes blooming like flowers on the walls and bookshelves full of my favourite books (Silver Snaffles, A Pony for Jean, Moorland Mousie, etc) and framed photographs of her ponies. The rain had stopped and a nearly full moon was shining in through the windows (I had drawn the curtains back as soon as Elizabeth left) and I could see without lifting my head from the pillow the silver hump of the down above the garden. I thought of the man who was now a sarcophagus riding across his downs and how he must have thought of them the night before the battle, before Henry the Fifth roused him with that glorious speech (or was that Shakespeare talking, and Laurence Olivier proclaiming?) and I thought of all the soldiers who died so far from home, and of John's body lying undiscovered for so long in that silent German wood, and I started to cry again.

"Overwrought," I could hear Jonesy saying. "It's her age."

I went to sleep, crying, thinking of John.

In the morning all my morbid thoughts had evaporated and I awoke feeling right back to normal. I had completely forgotten that ghastly Annabel would be coming to ride and my quite normal rage of jealousy sprang back immediately. What a stupid twerp I had been last night when I had had Con all to myself and all I could do was sniffle with self-pity! He must have been really fed up with me. What a super chance I had had to impress him! Certainly my brain had been completely addled. It felt clear and sharp now

111

that all my opportunities had flown. I got out of bed and went to the window, and there below was Annabel arriving on her bicycle and Con going down the drive to meet her, swinging two headcollars. I waited to see if they fell into each other's arms, but was pleased to see that Con was quite cool. Annabel parked her bike by the fence and Con handed her one of the headcollars. She looked as if she were about to ride in Rotten Row and I could tell she was fluttering her eyelashes (she couldn't help it!) but Con went away down the field without bothering with her, calling the ponies. Wizard, I thought. Surely if he loved her he would have given her a kiss? They took the ponies away out of my sight to tack up but were soon back riding down the drive, Annabel on the chestnut and Con on the grey. Con did not seem to be taking any notice of Annabel, I was pleased to see. I also had to acknowledge that she was a most elegant and efficient rider: she looked fantastic on the beautiful chestnut. Was she impressing Con? He rode like most boys, not caring, rough by comparison but I was glad to see that he wasn't bothering to chat her up as he rode.

They took a track on to the down, and then as the ponies lengthened into a trot and gradually grew fainter over the great shoulder of rippling grass my jealous thoughts went off at a tangent and I was filled with an agonizing desire to be on a pony riding over those downs. Con or no Con, it didn't matter, just to ride one of those beautiful ponies over the great expanse of grass with the sea shining in the distance and the sky cloudless in heaven above. It shook me, this longing, and I stood in this stupor of want until Elizabeth came and told me she was running me a bath and did I want a boiled egg for breakfast?

I had forgotten how dirty I was, got quite used to it in fact, and was amazed to find the bathwater much higher than the stipulated five inches which we always kept to religiously in my law-abiding home. It came over my chest and was quite delicious. I couldn't remember ever having had a bath like it. At the same time it felt wicked, such was my programming. But the water was impressively dirty by the time I got out and I had to clean the brown high-water mark, by which time Elizabeth called up that my boiled egg was ready. My clothes had been dried and laid out for me so I pulled them on and ran downstairs. This luxurious living!

After I had eaten Elizabeth drove me back to camp and I was in time for another breakfast. Having last been seen in Con's arms, I had to explain in detail everything that had happened to me. Great disappointment ensued when they heard that no passion had occurred on the sofa in front of the fire and several girls, I could see, despised me for my poor handling of the situation. I knew I was hopeless but I couldn't help it. Immature, as Jonesy was always berating. My mother too.

Anne understood, at least.

"It was strange last night, thinking about it. It made me cry too, sitting in that church. It was awful. I felt so homesick."

"Yes, I felt homesick."

"It's all right now though."

The sun was shining and we were back at work, hoeing cabbages like the Jerries, because it was too wet to cut the barley. Annabel had come back when breakfast was nearly over but she didn't ask me anything about staying the night; she didn't say anything at all and seemed rather cross, which was a good sign. Everyone was dying for work to be over so that we could go down to town and meet the boys, and luckily Mr Paul let us off early, mainly because we all had such terrible blisters we couldn't really continue. He said we were useless and he'd have done better if he had agreed to take prisoners, but then --- amazingly --- he laughed and said we could come to his party on Saturday. Next year all the young men would be back and he could run the farm properly. Les and Cyril said, "He'll be lucky, the wages he pays."

I remembered I was going out with Duffer on Saturday but luckily Mr Pauls' party was going to be all day with lots of food at lunch-time, so that would be all right. But what about Con's party?

"It's on Sunday," Annabel said, when asked.

This was all very satisfactory. Annabel wouldn't come down to town; she said the boys were too common. I supposed she might have arranged something with Con but I didn't ask her. I didn't want to know. She asked me if I was going out with Duffer.

I said I was.

"He's a Jew," she said.

I hadn't noticed.

"He's nice."

She gave me a pitying look. Sometimes I couldn't understand Annabel.

We were all a bit early in town as it was still working hours, so we mooched around the shops. Anne and I found a nice bookshop and browsed happily. I found a poor little benighted German book amongst the novels and it was so beautifully bound and very cheap I bought it on an impulse as a present for Rupert who had no family left. It was by some one called Thomas Mann who sounded English but was apparently German. I hoped he wasn't a Nazi, but the bookseller assured me he had moved to America in nineteen thirty nine and was a Nobel prize winner, so I thought those credentials were very sound. It was called Buddenbrooks. Of course I had no idea what it was about.

Then Anne and I went and sat on the beach, at least on the wall looking at the sea. By looking very hard we thought we could see France, but then we decided it was our imagination. Les and Cyril said they had actually heard the guns from over there during the war but we weren't sure whether to believe them. Our school was arranging exchange visits for us to visit France next summer and we had all been allocated pen-friends in Paris to start making our acquaintances. Mine was called Simone and from her photo looked about twenty-five. I had sent her a photo of myself in Girl Guide uniform which I realised already was a mistake. My mother was getting nervous already and it was still a year away. The waves were breaking peacefully on the beach and we sat lulled by the rhythmic murmuring, grateful for the great expanse of the Channel that had saved us from Hitler. The sun was shining now and we sat there with our throbbing hands feeling at peace with the world. You could always feel like this with Anne, not with anyone else the same. I supposed it was because she was religious.

After a bit the boys started to filter in our direction and Duffer came and sat with us. He saw my book and told me it was good. He had read it in the original German.

"We lived in Germany until ninety thirty eight. Luckily my parents saw the light in time and came here."

His English was so good I had never thought he was a foreigner. We had quite a lot of Jewish girls at our school who had come from Germany with their families before war broke out. They were mostly very clever. We took them for granted. I felt rather like this with Duffer. He was just nice, but he did not make my heart beat faster like Con did. He was a bit short, with spectacles, dark and earnest, a bit too earnest. But not boring at all. And his friends were a laugh. They all went to the same school. When they came we just messed about as usual and bought Tizer and sherbet with liquorice pipes until it was time to go back for supper. Les and Cyril had come down on the tractor and gave Anne and me a lift back, which was quite difficult, four on a tractor, especially as Les was a bit drunk. I sat on his lap and he kept biting my ear. I was quite relieved when we made it safely.

Annabel wasn't at supper. Some one said she had gone out with Con. This made me very fed up and although we had a sing song in the evening round a lovely big fire I kept thinking of Annabel and Con walking hand in hand in the moonlight somewhere and it made me sad.

115

FOURTEEN

The next day, Saturday, the day of Mr Paul's party, we had to do three hours stooking first to please the old skinflint and then we were let loose in the big field behind the farm buildings where the tables had been set up and the food (such as it was) and drink was laid out. We found that most of the visitors were neighbours and local farmers, a lot of them quite ancient and they took the places near the farm and the rest of us hangers-on rambled up the hillside and lay in the sun and sent forays down for snacks. Les and Cyril were up there with some local farm workers and we were surprised to find a little clique of German prisoners including Herman and Rupert. Had old Paul invited them, I wondered? They had brought their own beer and sat on a right of way that ran across the hillside so technically Mr Paul could not order them off. I remembered my little German book and went all the way back to camp to fetch it. Rupert was sitting a little apart with Herman and I felt really stupid approaching him with my gift. His English was hopeless, so I didn't know what to say. I just sort of thrust it at him and mumbled, "I bought you a present." He took it and looked at it carefully, then at me, and to my horror burst into tears.

I had never seen a man cry before. I didn't know they could. I was shocked and felt terrible. What had I done? I looked at Herman helplessly, and he said, "Your kindness --- it undoes him." He put his arm round poor Rupert, like a great bear protecting its young, and murmured soft German things to him, and in a minute Rupert hiccuped and gave a watery smile, and then he put out a hand and shook mine very warmly, as if we had just been introduced, and said, "Bitte, bitte, bitte, mein Fraulein."

This incident shook me. I stumbled back to the farm and lay in a barn full of hay, wanting to be on my own.. It was very hot now and below me in the yard all the old ladies were gossiping away surrounded by hens and ducks picking up their crumbs, and the old men were gathered in groups talking shop and drinking a lot of beer. Through the windows of the farmhouse a tinny old gramophone was playing elderly music. All my friends were there except Annabel. No doubt she was off somewhere with Con. Whenever anyone asked her about Con she just smiled in her

superior way and kept her silence. She managed to put all her hours in at work and was very good at stooking --- hers never fell down --- but after work she disappeared. She had never been down to town with us, mixing with the 'common boys' ; she wasn't into fun, not our sort anyway. She wasn't like the rest of us. I knew I was going out with Duffer later and I really liked Duffer. It is hadn't been for Con I would have been really excited about the evening ahead, but as it was I could only think about Con. He made my heart jump about just thinking about him. Duffer didn't have the same effect somehow, in spite of being so nice. Tomorrow the party was going to be at Con's house and then I would see him again, but no doubt Annabel would appropriate him and that was that.

So I went out with Duffer. He had borrowed a car for the occasion, a funny little heap, but it got us to Brighton where we went to the cinema and saw "The Way to the Stars". I had already seen it at home but I didn't tell Duffer, and I didn't mind seeing it again as it was such a beautiful film, all about bombing Germany. Terribly sad. I cried again although I knew what was going to happen, and Duffer touched my hand a bit, not really holding it, just touching my fingers. Afterwards we went for fish and ships and ate them on on the prom, looking at the sea. It was very pleasant, just the two of us, and it was quiet where we were although we could hear celebrations in the distance. But it wasn't late, just the dusk coming and the red sun slowly slipping towards the horizon where the first buoy was starting to blink. Duffer told me about his family, and that his grandparents had been taken away by the Gestapo and now they didn't know what had happened to them, and perhaps they never would. He said his mother cried a lot. I thought that if I had been her I would have too. After seeing the film, and hearing about Duffer's grandparents, I felt very sad and as the sun started to disappear into the sea I wanted to think that the sadness was over and when it came up again on the other side it would be a new world where everything was all right again. A bit daft really, because how could it change for the people whose family had been killed and would never come back again? John's aunt and uncle, so jokey and kind, had aged irreparably. And Rupert . . .

Seeing my glum face Duffer said, "I shouldn't have told you all this, I'm sorry. We're
supposed to be enjoying ourselves. Shall we drive out and walk on the cliffs? Or would you like to come home with me? My parents won't mind."

In the end we drove back to his home but we didn't go in. We went and met all the others down by the sea, and had cups of tea and more chips and then he drove eight of us back to camp in the car which was very funny. We had to be in by ten to placate Jonesy and Piggy. We were half an hour late but Jonesy and Piggy didn't seem to mind. They were rather giggly and by then we were all giggly too, so we stumbled to our tents and Duffer drove away. The next day was Sunday, our day off, with Elizabeth's party which started at midday, so we could lie in if we wanted to. Some one suggested we sent a message down to the farm to say we wanted breakfast in bed but no one volunteered to go.

I had to recount my outing with Duffer and they were very disappointed that we hadn't kissed. "No wonder he's called Duffer," some one said. His real name was Aaron, I had found out.

Annabel came in when we were all nearly asleep. How did she manage to command her freedom the way she did without Jonesy or Piggy interfering?

I asked her. She said her father had written a letter to say he expected her to be allowed to do what she liked in her time off. It was his responsibility. Her father's letters were like commands from God: I suppose they were written on Buckingham Palace notepaper. Our school was very snobby: anyone who was on first names with the king was bound to be obeyed. Annabel was only in our tent because she was supposed to be a friend of mine and no one else liked her much. Anne was nice to everybody, and Joy was on another planet, dreaming of her home in Wyoming .

"Where've you been?"

"To a nightclub in Brighton."

"How did you get back?"

"In his car, of course."

I was disappointed. I didn't think Con was a nightclub type, although you never knew with those public school boys. They were very sophisticated, not like Peter and Duffer. All I knew about nightclubs was what I had seen in American films. I had rather been thinking that Con was like the sarcophagus man, a man of the fields with soldierly leanings, to fight for his country. This seemed to be very noble, not like a man who drank gin and danced. I knew that Annabel would appropriate him at tomorrow's party and I wouldn't stand a chance.

But as it turned out the star of the party was Con's Uncle Albert. Uncle Albert was the all-singing, all-dancing crackerjack of party-organizers: what a party he made! As we knew that the party was going to be more a family party for relatives and family friends and that we were only there out of kindness, as extras, we had expected something like Mr Paul's with the elderly aunts, etc, perhaps a bit of singing round the piano and charades and things. We put on our already greatly creased and smelly best clothes and decided to brave it out although I know most of us would secretly have preferred the 'banquet' Les and Cyril were presiding over in a secret field below the downs. Les had found a dead sheep and had skinned it and was going to cook it on a spit and had invited the German prisoners as well as the usual gang. It sounded really good. However we knew our duty and instead trooped obediently up the road to Elizabeth's stately home instead.

It was a beautiful day and the food was brilliant, mostly egg things as everyone around here kept hens. There were egg and tomato pies and egg and cress sandwiches and hard-boiled eggs with beetroot and celery and also plates of cold beef: Con had brought home half a dead calf from the farm where he worked; it had a better provenance than Les's sheep, no doubt, and nobody asked any questions. Con was there chatting up Annabel and in fact being nice to all of us in his well-brought-up way although I could see he thought this sort of party was a bit of a bore after all his night-clubbing. He still made me feel funny when I looked at him, I couldn't help it. I hated Annabel so much, always taking what I wanted.

After lunch Uncle Albert decided on sports: first, a three-legged race. He chose the pairs. I was roped up to eighty-year-old auntie Eileen and Con got a two-year-old toddler cousin. Annabel got an arthritic farmer and Anne got the vicar. Auntie Eileen and I were third from last. I must say she was really game but I was terrified she would fall over and have a heart attack. The wheelbarrow race was only for the young and able-bodied and very competitive it turned out to be. I longed to have Con holding my ankles but he teamed up with Annabel and won (of course) and I got Joy who was hopeless (I couldn't see her being much good on the ranch if she couldn't even do a wheelbarrow race). After that all the men carried the piano out on to the lawn and Uncle Albert sat down and played all the stupid things like Run Rabbit Run Rabbit Run Run Run and Roll

Out the Barrel which we could all bawl out quite happily and then he started on the Hokey Cokey. We danced this until we were all totally conked out but still shouting for more.

"You put your right leg in.
Your put your right leg out,

You put your right leg in and shake it all about.

Hey, hokey hokey cokey!

Hey hokey hokey cokey! etc, etc.

It was always good for a laugh but that night it must have been heard all the way to Brighton the way Uncle Albert inspired us. We sang and danced in this frenetic circle, arms round each other, in and out, backwards and forwards, sweating, laughing, falling about until we could dance no more. Then we lay in the grass laughing and giggling and Elizabeth brought out great jugs of water (the lemonade had run out) and the sun started to go down with a great golden flush in the sky over the downs. I lay on my back in the warm grass smelling its lovely scent and listening to the blackbirds singing their evening songs in the rhododendron bushes and I felt gorged with happiness. All the terrible things were over and nothing would be sad again, I thought, not now the war was over. The ghost of the sarcophagus man was riding over the crest of the downs, happy with his duty done and his lovely land still inviolate, bearing its crops and flowers for ever. The sky was full of gnats and swallows and fading into a soft dusk, the colour of lilacs, then deeper, deeper.

"Hey, have you gone to sleep?"

I blinked, startled.

It was Con, hunkering down beside me.

"Once," he said, "Way back when we first met, I thought I heard you say you could ride."

"Yes, I can. A bit."

"Would you like to ride now?"

"What, me?" I thought he was joking.

"It's lovely when it's dark, over the downs. I thought you might like it."

"But . . . what about Annabel?"

"Who? Annabel?"

"Oh --- Gertrude."

"She just comes in the morning. She's not for

evenings."

I rather thought she was. I suppose he meant on a horse. I was knocked sideways by this proposition and could scarcely believe it was happening.

"Come on."

I got up slowly. My head was reeling. The Hokey Cokey had knocked all the stuffing out of me. I followed Con across the lawn, unseeing. We went to the stables and he unhooked the bridles and said, "It'll be better bareback. You've got a skirt, useless with a saddle. You're all right bareback?"

"Yes, of course." I had often ridden Dolly bareback.

"We'll go round behind the hedge and no one'll see us. Ma will interfere if she guesses what we're doing."

I couldn't believe this was happening. Like the sarcophagus man I was going to ride into the sunset over the downs. Did he ride with his lady, I wondered? Were we his ghosts? I felt like a ghost. When I thought I was happy a few minutes earlier, it was as nothing to how I felt now.

"Sirdar, the grey, is easier. You can ride him. We can just walk, if you like. Get a bit of peace. Uncle Albert's parties are always a bit much."

The chatter and laughter of the party died away as we came out from behind the shrubbery on to the drive and to the gate into the field. The sun was just disappearing over the side of the hill and the sky was a great flush of gold and violet as if to celebrate my amazing fortune. The ponies came towards us, trailing black shadows, silhouetted against the sunset. I had to squint to see which was which. Annabel always rode the chestnut, the showy one. I was glad Con had given me the other.

We bridled them and Con gave me a leg up. I tried to arrange my skirt in a ladylike manner but it rode up, showing all my bare brown legs. I wore my useful grey shorts every day and now, just when I needed them, I was in a stupid skirt. Con was in shorts and his once clean white shirt was all grass stains from the wheelbarrow race. We hardly measured up to the elegance of our mounts . . . who was this mythical Deirdre who had the fortune to own two such glorious animals?

"She's gone away on a course, jumping cross-country, on Exmoor somewhere. It's all she thinks about, horses. She's batty. I don't mind just riding about, like this --- saving the legs --- but not all that competition stuff. Like now, it's nice."

We went down the drive and along the road a little way and then on to a soft grassy bridleway that curved away up on to the downs. We just walked idly and the ponies were relaxed, even the fizzy chestnut. He was called Red Admiral and was a star jumper, Con said.

"Your Gertrude likes him best. He shows her off."

I digested this remark, feeling hopefully that it was slightly derogative.

"She's a very good rider," I said, nobly generous.

"Yes. She's okay."

"Are you going out with her later?"

He looked surprised. "No. Why should I?"

"I thought she went out with you in the evenings. She goes out every night and comes back late. She doesn't say who with. We all supposed it was you."

Con laughed.

"She suggested it, I remember. She's got a cousin who runs a night club in Brighton, but I said it wasn't my scene. She said her cousin would let us in for nothing and give us free drinks but I wasn't persuaded. So she goes down there to see him every night. She's okay for helping with the exercising, but not for anything else. I think she's pretty ghastly, to tell you the truth."

"Yes, so do I."

My voice came out very cool. But I could feel great waves of glory flooding me at these fantastic revelations.

It wasn't Con that Annabel went out with! He didn't even like her!! Her

eyelash-fluttering had made no impact on this delectable down-to-earth country boy, my heart's

delight. He was smiling at me in the dusk as if he guessed my secret.

"I would rather take you out."

"What, to a night club?" I tried to keep the apprehension out of my voice.

"No. This sort of thing, what we're doing now."

"Oh yes!"

I felt myself swooning with delight. I could not believe such a wonderful thing was

happening to me. Just to ride this fabulous pony in this fabulous place was enough but to add the fabulous boy as well was almost too much. I was speechless. We were coming round the long curve of the green lane to where it gave out on to the great expanse of chalky down where the turf was hundreds of years old and speckled in the dusk with a myriad flowers. No wartime plough had touched it; the same flowers had nodded to the passing hooves of the knight's horse as he surveyed his domain. How could Con possibly want to leave all this and join the army, I wondered, as our ponies shouldered up the steep path? Was he just the same as his ancestor, bored with privilege, wanting excitement in his life? When John had chosen flying, had he wanted to be up there in the stars, out of humdrum life? But it never turned out that way, couldn't they see? Not for the sarcophagus man, nor for Con's brother, nor for John, nor for all the millions and millions who had died in battle.

Gosh, was I getting delirious, these philosophies flooding my brainbox, my mind turned by the joy that coursed through my bloodstream as the lovely pony beneath me breasted the crest of the downs?

The whole world was spread below us, all the lights of Brighton, released from the years of darkness, glittering, with fountains of fireworks here and there reaching up, springs of delight. And beyond, the inscrutable darkness of the sea with the occasional faint blink of a distant buoy.

Con turned back, laughing.

"Do you like it?"

He guessed that my suburban upbringing had never prepared me for this panorama.

"It's wonderful!"

"Shall we canter? In the dark --- it's amazing --- you'll see. Are you okay, bareback?"

"Yes! Yes!"

Ahead of me the chestnut pony's tail swirled out in sudden movement. My pony's stride lengthened, smooth, so smooth, the perfect pony that I had dreamed of all my life, the warm shoulders sliding rhythmically before me and the soft caress of his hooves over the ancient turf . . . above me a great canopy of dusk-violet sky where the first stars were faint, not yet competing with the spectacle below. What more could I want? Could I ever want? On top of the whole world, the lights beckoning and the stride lengthening, faster and faster, chasing the wonderful boy across the arc of the downs, into the night.

THE END

AFTERWORD

No one seems to know whether this is a novel or a memoir. To tell the truth I am a bit confused myself.

About five years ago I wrote a novel (definitely a novel) called *Blue Skies and Gunfire* in which I drew on the memories of my childhood in the suburbs of London during the war. When I had finished it ~ a purely imaginary story ~ I found that the stirring of those memories was prompting me to write more about this period of my life. I decided on a more auto-biographical format and set off happily telling the truth. If I strayed into fiction here and there I don't think it shows and it certainly doesn't matter. A book is a book.

But for the record (editor's request): all the people are true and unadorned (Annabel possibly a little exaggerated) and everything that happens is true with one or two exceptions. John, incredibly, survived the war; it was his brother, who lived next door and was also in bombers, who was killed. John didn't come to the dance and nor did the GIs and Con, alas, didn't exist, so although we all went to the thanksgiving in the church and I remember thinking exactly those thoughts about all the soldiers who were remembered in the brass plaques and monuments, I didn't faint and unfortunately never experienced the bliss of a hot bath in the house of the kindly 'old gel' up the road.

And did Joy marry her GI? I never found out. A new world opened up with the ending of the war and we all went our different ways.

Kathleen Peyton, 2012